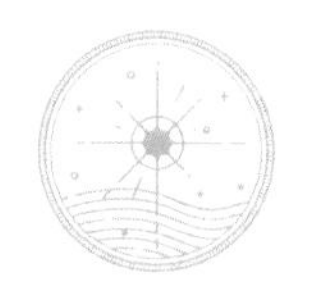

# LIVING **CHRIST**

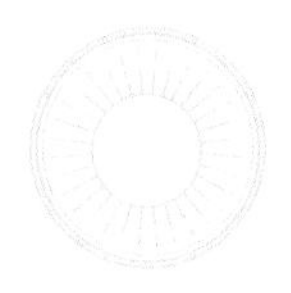

EMBODYING **JESUS'** LIFE IN **WORSHIP**
THROUGH THE **CHRISTIAN YEAR**

DANIEL L. **RIFE**

wesleyan
PUBLISHING HOUSE
wphstore.com
Indianapolis, Indiana

Published by Wesleyan Publishing House
Indianapolis, Indiana 46250
Printed in the United States of America
ISBN: 978-1-63257-346-9
ISBN (e-book): 978-1-63257-347-6

Library of Congress Cataloging-in-Publication Data

Names: Rife, Daniel L., 1989- author.
Title: Living Christ : embodying Jesus' life in worship through the Christian year / Daniel L. Rife.
Description: Indianapolis, Indiana : Wesleyan Publishing House, 2020. | Includes bibliographical references. | Summary: "Living Christ is not a historical exposition nor is it a rule book. It is a resource that will inspire you to allow Christ to permeate your preparation for worship-whether you're a worship planner leading a community or a person seeking to establish sacred rhythms in your personal life. Organized over the course of a Christian year, Author Daniel Rife offers practical and accessible ways to incorporate a deeper fellowship with Christ"-- Provided by publisher.
Identifiers: LCCN 2020001913 (print) | LCCN 2020001914 (ebook) | ISBN 9781632573469 (paperback) | ISBN 9781632573476 (ebook)
Subjects: LCSH: Worship. | Liturgies. | Spiritual life--Christianity. | Church year.
Classification: LCC BV10.3 .R54 2020 (print) | LCC BV10.3 (ebook) | DDC 263/.9--dc23
LC record available at https://lccn.loc.gov/2020001913
LC ebook record available at https://lccn.loc.gov/2020001914

To my parents,

who instilled in me wonder and creativity;

to my colleague and friend, Emily Vermilya,

who introduced me to the Christian Year;

to my wife, Jordan,

who manifests the Christian Year in our church and community;

and to the people of College Wesleyan Church,

who played a premier role in forming this resource and me.

# CONTENTS

# INTRODUCTION

## Why a Book about the Christian Year?

Every worship service tells a story. But what story is it? Whose story is it? And what type of person is that story forming us into? Could it be possible that we are unaware of what story we're telling each Sunday, and therefore unintentional in how our congregation is being formed by our worship practices? But what if we *were* aware? What if we *could* be intentional? For Christian worship, by its name alone, is called to tell one story: the story of the living Christ.

This isn't as easy as it sounds. I've been a worship practitioner just under a decade and still have to fight the temptation to include certain songs, elements, or people just because I can. It's easy to get swept up in the hype, the emotion, and the intellect of popular Christian culture. But as soon as the purpose of Christian worship digresses from telling the story of Christ to our own motives and aspirations, we have lost the very center of our existence. Therefore, this book is my attempt to offer a method by which worship planners can reorient their weekly services to accomplish that ultimate goal—telling the story of Christ.

There are numerous ways a church could remember and celebrate the life of Christ in worship. So, please, do not consider this book prescriptive. Nor should you consider it a historical exposition. There are many excellent authors, more qualified than I, who can explain the historical background and traditions mentioned in this book. I've included a list of them in the bibliography. So, this is neither a history book nor a rule book. I do hope, though, that it is an inspiring book—one that stirs in you new ideas of how the life of Christ might permeate your own life and the worshiping life of your context.

This book is for the current and future worship planner who wants to center a community on the life of Christ. Whether you are a senior pastor, worship leader, ministry leader, or student in training, I hope this book will offer accessible and practical ways to corporately live Christ's life over the course of a year. Though many of the examples offered in this book lend themselves to the Sunday morning service, several of the ideas could easily translate to age-specific ministries, small groups and Sunday schools, or even the family living room. For the layperson who just wants a simple introduction to the Christian Year or the person seeking to establish sacred rhythms in their own life, I hope that—between the more instructional sections—this book will pass on the essence of Christ's life and invite you to deeper fellowship with him.

Each chapter is ascribed to a particular season of the Christian Year—which I'll explain more in depth in the following pages. Beneath the chapter header you will find a short description of the time frame of the season within the year, its associated symbolic color, as well as any special days to note. Within the introduction of the season you will find a schedule of readings from what is known as the Revised Common Lectionary.[1] Every Sunday and some special days are assigned a reading from the Old Testament, the Psalms, the Gospels, and the Epistles. As I mentioned earlier, I offer these not as prescriptions but inspiration. These assigned readings match the particular season of the Christian Year in either content or theme and can therefore be immensely helpful in bringing focus to your service planning. After giving a brief overview, I offer a couple possibilities as to how you might join the spirit of the season. I conclude each chapter with a list of either a special focus you might promote, or special services you might consider offering your congregation in the particular season.

The final chapter, "Telling Christ's Story beyond the Sunday Gathering," is perhaps the most instructive within the whole book. The

Christian Year has multiple special days on which it is appropriate to offer a corporate worship service in addition to the weekly gathering of believers. Planning a service that isn't confined to a regular order of worship can sometimes be overwhelming. This chapter offers some methods for planning special services, as well as multiple service outlines for you and your team to either contextualize for your own people or inspire you to create your own original services.

Whether you read the whole book at once or read each chapter separately as you prepare for an upcoming season or plan a special service, I hope that you come back to this book time and time again. The story stays the same, but we don't. Our lives are ever-changing—our relationships and our work is often filled with new trials and adventures. But, year after year, as we continue to return to Christ, who is our life, we learn to see the things he sees; we learn to hear the things he hears; we might even find ourselves doing the things he does—and we join God's testimony in saying, "He has given us eternal life, and this life is in his Son" (1 John 5:11).

## CALENDARS

Everything we do is making us into someone. What we eat, how much we sleep, the people we interact with in our communities, what we do with our free time—we are but the result of choices we've made and the habits we've grown accustomed to. Whether we literally write them down or not, it is these choices and habits that make up our calendar. So, if you were to show me your schedule, I could probably tell you what you value, because we make time for what's important to us. Whether it's actually the meeting we value or the job we'll lose if we don't attend the meeting, our calendars reveal a lot about our value system.

If I were to replace your calendar with my calendar, and you went to all my appointments, met all my deadlines, and celebrated all the birthdays of people close to me, your life would eventually look a lot more like mine than yours. Even on a physical level, if I took on the calendar of an Olympic athlete, my arms might actually fill my sleeves and I might not be as self-conscious at the pool. Calendars reveal a lot about us, because it is not enough for me to simply say, "I want to be an astronaut." I have to make time to do the things that astronauts in training do. If I don't, then I won't be an astronaut.

So, if this argument stands, it is not enough to simply say, "I want to be like Christ." Rather, we must integrate Christ's calendar into our own lives—his habits, special events, conversations, the journeys, the waiting, the meals, and so on. If we do this, in time, our lives will begin to look like his. And eventually, if we consistently enact the habits of Jesus, we would likely no longer be copying him; instead, we might actually take on his values. When we live the life of Christ—that is, when we are *living* Christ—we become like him. Thomas Howard, in his book *Evangelical Is Not Enough*, writes,

> There is a profound mystery at work here, touching on the threefold sense in which the gospel is true for Christian believers. Everything recorded in the Gospels happened once in actual history; but these events must be translated by the Holy Ghost into the Christian's own life (Christ must be born in us; we must be circumcised in the inner man; we must be crucified with Him and raised with Him and ascend with Him); and, thirdly, we must perpetually keep coming back in our minds to these events, marking and remembering them, and meditating on them.[2]

This is salvation: not one single moment, but the summation of a life characterized by Christ's birth, death, and resurrection in the choices, habits, sacrifices, and relationships of a person. The more we learn to integrate our calendar into Christ's calendar, the more we might discover how Christ would live our life.

## THE CHRISTIAN YEAR

The Christian Year or Calendar (Liturgical Year or Calendar) is a historic method of remembering Christ's life on earth. Just as you might divide your own life into seasons of childhood, teenage years, college days, and early, middle, and late adult life, Christ's life is likewise remembered in six seasons. In **Advent**, we remember the expectation of his arrival; in **Christmas**, his birth; in **Epiphany**, we see him grow up and begin his ministry; in **Lent**, his journey to death; in **Easter** (spoiler alert), we see him live again; and in **Ordinary Time**, we see his church established.

Chances are, even those who have never heard of the Christian Year still celebrate it in part. Christmas and Easter are perhaps the most commonly celebrated days of the Christian Year. However, as seen above, they are not just singular days but entire seasons. In fact, the entire Christian Year can be divided into two cycles: the **Christmas Cycle** (Advent, Christmas, and Epiphany) and the **Easter Cycle** (Lent, Easter, and Ordinary Time). Both cycles have a season of preparation, then a season of realization, and end with a season of implication.

In reference to the actual length of time of the seasons, the Christian Year can be divided into two parts of revelation and response. Close to six months (December through March/April) focus on the revelation of God in the man Jesus Christ (Advent, Christmas, Epiphany, Lent, and Easter), while the last six months (May/June through November) focus on the response of the church to go and make disciples (Ordinary Time). It is appropriate that this annual calendar follows the model of divine dialogue as this pattern of revelation and response is consistent with God's activity throughout the biblical narrative.[3]

Though each season has a title, more important is the ethos or disposition of the season. In a way, Christ even teaches us emotional competency as we journey with him through excitement, joy, determination, pain, and sorrow—all very real human emotions that a church may not regularly focus on. So, you will see that each season is titled not only with the traditional label, but also an invitation that encapsulates the ethos of that particular time within the Christian Year. Just as a sonata—a specific type of classical music composition—is made up of different movements, the life of Christ is made up of narrative movements that, when performed in succession, complete the work. These movements are:

- **Advent:** The Invitation to Anticipate Christ's Coming
- **Christmas:** The Invitation to Celebrate Christ's Presence on Earth
- **Epiphany:** The Invitation to Wonder at Christ's Work on Earth
- **Lent:** The Invitation to Reckon Our Life with Christ's Life and Death
- **Easter:** The Invitation to Triumph with Christ over Sin and Death
- **Ordinary Time:** The Invitation to Commit to Christ through the Church

Similar to a musical composition, one living the Christian Year will experience the evolution of rhythmic variations, the emergence of dynamic differentiation, a mélange of textures and forms, with cascading melodies that diversify into complex harmonies, fluctuating keys, skipping from consonance to dissonance, while never losing the original motif. In the simplest terms: the Christian Year is a journey. Things will change along the way—things as simple as colors, symbols, dispositions, and main supporting characters—but God's original purpose never changes: redemption for all of creation through the life of Christ.

In his book *You Are What You Love*, James K. A. Smith argues the premise of his title by quoting Antoine de Saint-Exupéry, writing, "If you want to build a ship, don't drum up people to collect wood and don't assign them tasks and work, but rather teach them to long for the endless immensity of the sea."[4] This is the goal of Christian worship, not to simply call people to tasks and work, but to teach them to long for the endless immensity of Christ. Building a ship is second nature to someone who values the sea. Perhaps the pursuit of Christ would bear in us a new nature entirely. So, I invite you on this journey of embodying Christ's life in worship. May you know him more as you walk with him and may you be "filled with the fruit of righteousness, which comes from Jesus Christ, in order to give glory and praise to God" (Phil. 1:11 CEB).

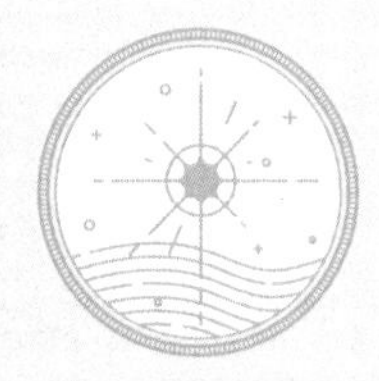

# ADVENT

## The Invitation to Anticipate Christ's Coming

### TIME

4 weeks
*beginning on the fourth Sunday before December 25 through December 24*

### COLOR

Blue
*(color of hope)*
or purple
*(color of penitence and royalty)*

### SPECIAL DAYS

- **Gaudete Sunday** (the third Sunday of Advent)
- **Christmas Eve** (December 24)

The story begins, as many ancient stories do, *in medias res* (in the midst of things). Prophecies of a major plot twist are announced, and anticipation rises. The Creator of all things is stepping into the time and space of his creation. Isaiah announces, "Be strong, and do not fear, for your God is coming to destroy your enemies. He is coming to save you" (Isa. 35:4). Isaiah is echoed by Jeremiah, Micah, Zephaniah, and Malachi. Something new is about to happen that neither Israel nor the world fully understands. Hope is ignited, peace is promised, joy is alive, and love has a name.

In the reenactment of the season of Advent each year, the church emerges from the previous year's prolonged season of Ordinary Time. Throughout Ordinary Time, we have become more aware of and burdened by the brokenness around us and even *in* us. We join the psalmist in crying out, "O LORD, how long will you forget me? Forever? How long will you look the other way?" (13:1). But we have hope: "The day will come, says the LORD, when I will do for Israel and Judah all the good things I have promised them" (Jer. 33:14). "At just the right time God's voice breaks into the ordinary, "Look, I am making everything new!" (Rev. 21:5). "Comfort, comfort my people" (Isa. 40:1). And yet, God does not simply pull his people out of the darkness. Rather, the Light steps into the darkness in the form of a weak, vulnerable, and dependent newborn baby. God took on the likeness of humanity, so humanity could take on the likeness of God.[1]

Advent is a season of liminality—a transition period. We join the ancient cries of Israel longing for a Savior, and yet we live in the time after the revelation of the Christ. On this side of the incarnation, we not only remember Christ's first coming, but we also look forward to his second coming. Therefore, it is appropriate to merge these two narratives. Though they occupy different spaces of cosmic time, they both reveal a Creator that identifies with his creation and has not left us alone; one who promises to wipe every tear from our eyes and make all things new.

| | YEAR A | YEAR B | YEAR C |
|---|---|---|---|
| WEEK 1 | Isaiah 2:1–5<br>Psalm 122<br>Romans 13:11–14<br>Matthew 24:36–44 | Isaiah 64:1–9<br>Psalm 80:1–7, 17–19<br>1 Corinthians 1:3–9<br>Mark 13:24–37 | Jeremiah 33:14–16<br>Psalm 25:1–10<br>1 Thessalonians 3:9–13<br>Luke 21:25–36 |
| WEEK 2 | Isaiah 11:1–10<br>Psalm 72:1–7, 18–19<br>Romans 15:4–13<br>Matthew 3:1–12 | Isaiah 40:1–11<br>Psalm 85:1–2, 8–13<br>2 Peter 3:8–15a<br>Mark 1:1–8 | Malachi 3:1–4<br>Luke 1:68–79<br>Philippians 1:3–11<br>Luke 3:1–6 |
| WEEK 3 | Isaiah 35:1–10<br>Psalm 146:5–10<br>*or* Luke 1:46b–55<br>James 5:7–10<br>Matthew 11:2–11 | Isaiah 61:1–4, 8–11<br>Psalm 126<br>*or* Luke 1:46b–55<br>1 Thessalonians 5:16–24<br>John 1:6–8, 19–28 | Zephaniah 3:14–20<br>Isaiah 12:2–6<br>Philippians 4:4–7<br>Luke 3:7–18 |
| WEEK 4 | Isaiah 7:10–16<br>Psalm 80:1–7, 17–19<br>Romans 1:1–7<br>Matthew 1:18–25 | 2 Samuel 7:1–11, 16<br>Luke 1:46b–55<br>*or* Psalm 89:1–4, 19–26<br>Romans 16:25–27<br>Luke 1:26–38 | Micah 5:2–5a<br>Luke 1:46b–55<br>*or* Psalm 80:1–7<br>Hebrews 10:5–10<br>Luke 1:39–45 (46–55) |

Parenthesis used in the assigned psalm indicate a shorter selection of verses that could be read in place of the entire psalm. Parenthesis used in all other references indicate optional additional verses that could be included with the assigned readings.

Blue or purple are the colors used to signify this season. Purple has been traditionally used in Advent, and blue is a more recent addition to the Christian Year color scheme, offering a unique expression of the season. Blue is the color of hope, while purple (also used in Lent) is the color of both penitence and royalty. Both colors are appropriate for Advent. We are penitent as our heavenly King takes on human form, yet we are hopeful for his presence and salvation. Coming from a tradition that emphasizes the hope of transformation, we are inclined toward the use of blue during this season. But remember, you are seeking to retell the story of Christ in your context; to get stuck on what color should or shouldn't signify a season is to misunderstand the color's function. The color your context uses is a backdrop to the season—setting the scene for this part of the story and developing an ethos for this specific movement within the entirety of Christ's sonata.

Two days stand out in this four-week-long season: the midpoint and the end. In the middle of the season, the church celebrates **Gaudete Sunday** (gäo͞odetā), or in English "Rejoice!" If you have ever witnessed the lighting of an Advent wreath, you may have noticed a pink candle among three blue (or purple) candles. No, the church staff didn't just run out of one color of candles. On the third week of the season of Advent, a pink candle is lit in contrast to the other candles lit on weeks one, two, and four. This is because the ethos shifts on this third Sunday from an anticipation grounded in promise to an anticipation grounded in realization, therefore, we rejoice!

The second day that stands out in Advent is the final day of the season: **Christmas Eve**, December 24. Many congregations will gather together on this day to welcome the season of Christmas. Many evangelical churches don't offer a service on Christmas Day, and it is not uncommon for some evangelical churches to cancel services when December 25 does align with a Sunday. Therefore, Christmas Eve can be a formative service for your people to commemorate at the end of four long weeks of waiting, inviting them into the celebration of Christmas.

## WAYS TO JOIN THE ANTICIPATION OF ADVENT

### ADVENT WREATH

A common tradition of the church is to place four candles along the border of a wreath on the altar (three blue or purple, and one pink). Each week one additional candle is lit so that, on the final Sunday of Advent, all four candles are burning. You might choose to include an additional larger white candle in the center of the wreath to be lit on Christmas Eve or on the first Sunday of Christmas. This candle is often called the Christ candle. If the Christ candle regularly sits on the altar in your context, the story of the Christian Year can interact with it on a couple different occasions, as it represents the light Christ brought into the world.

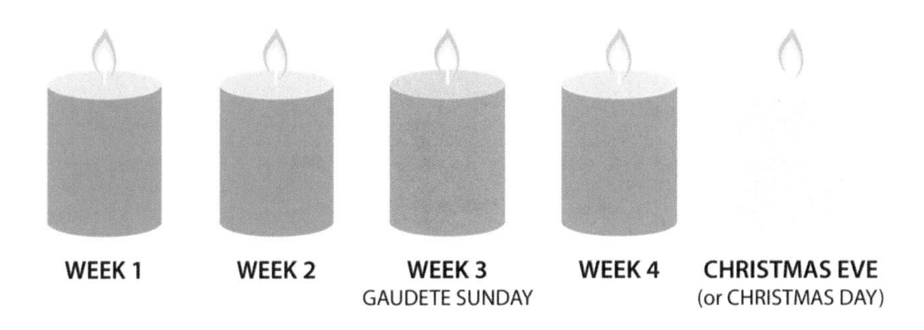


During Sunday services in Advent, you may choose to simply have the appropriate candles already lit, or you could include a time to light the candles within the service. Many traditions will include a verse of Scripture or song to be paired with this element. You could include a portion of the assigned lectionary texts for these days. You could have different congregation members offer testimonies each week about a time they waited on something from

God, perhaps without ever sharing if they received it, concluding with a scriptural affirmation of God's nature. Perhaps you could use an Old Testament prophecy to remember Israel's waiting for Christ's first coming and a New Testament exhortation to anticipate his second coming. You could even use an Old Testament text about Christ's first coming to encourage your congregation as you anticipate Christ's second coming. Imagine, for example, pairing James 5 with Isaiah 40:

**EPISTLE:** Dear brothers and sisters, be patient as you wait for the Lord's return. Consider the farmers who patiently wait for the rains in the fall and in the spring. They eagerly look for the valuable harvest to ripen. You, too, must be patient. Take courage, for the coming of the Lord is near.

—James 5:7–8

**PROPHECY:** "Comfort, comfort my people,"
says your God.
"Speak tenderly to Jerusalem.
Tell her that her sad days are gone
and her sins are pardoned.
Yes, the Lord has punished her twice
over for all her sins."

Listen! It's the voice of someone shouting,
"Clear the way through the wilderness
for the Lord!
Make a straight highway through the
wasteland for our God!"

—Isaiah 40:1–3

After these readings, a testimony, or a song, the appropriate candle can be lit. Depending on your context, a bell could be rung while the candle is lit to enhance this element. The ringing of a bell is a historic symbol. It is a "joyful noise" that calls our attention to Christ's mysterious presence, often rung in correlation to the eucharistic prayer. Just as a candle is lit to symbolize the coming of the Light, a bell can toll to symbolize the ever-presence of God among us as we wait for the return of the incarnate Christ. This element is an excellent opportunity to include small groups or families in your services as well. Each week, the readings could be divided between different readers, while another person lights the candle and another rings the bell.

## PRACTICE SILENCE AND WAITING

With the use of Scripture, we can tell the story of Israel's waiting and make connections of their yearning with our own lives. Yet, so often, our services are filled instead with elements to be accomplished—every second is accounted for, and any moment absent of activity causes people to wonder, "What's going on? Did someone miss their cue?" The season of Advent teaches us that something is happening in the waiting, in the longing, in the silence—that even nothing is indeed something. Advent reminds us that we can be confident, even hopeful, in waiting, anticipating the manifestation of God's redeeming work, as we quietly continue in faithfully living amidst his perceived silence.

Waiting is not a message the world teaches us. We are taught to take control, to act, to react. But it is often in waiting that our true heart shows through. When we are left without instruction, without control, without knowledge of what comes next, we might just find ourselves melting down our gold to create a god that will fill the silence (see Ex. 32). Counterculturally, Advent invites us to practice corporate waiting.

Explaining and incorporating regular moments of silence throughout the four Sundays is very appropriate. Perhaps silence could occur after the Advent readings to allow the congregation to center themselves within the gathering, maybe before the Scripture presentation or the sermon, as a preparation for the Word, or maybe after the sermon to consent to the Word. We are rarely taught to simply sit and wait, trusting that God can work even when we are not. This is a necessary practice and posture for the church as we seek to reenact the story of God. He does not move at our pace; often we must slow down to keep up with him.

## SPECIAL SERVICES

There are numerous opportunities to incorporate special services within the season of Advent, and the final chapter of this resource offers a collection of these services and others in greater depth. Here let me offer a bird's-eye view of some of the common Advent services. A **Hanging of the Greens** service is a service of preparation, as the church is decorated for the season throughout the service—each decoration symbolizing a portion of the larger story. Amidst the season you might consider including a service of **Lessons and Carols**: a conglomeration of Scripture texts (lessons) and carols paired to retell the story in simple revelation and response pattern. You could use the **O Antiphons**, the names of the promised Savior used in the carol "O Come, O Come, Emmanuel," to structure a service of hope. The United Methodist Church even has a service order for an Advent service of lament called "**A Blue Christmas**," for those who—because of loss or suffering—find the season more painful than hopeful.

Advent ends on Christmas Eve and is often commemorated with a **Christmas Eve service**. This service acts as a doorway into the celebration of Christmas and sometimes actually goes through midnight when the season of Christmas is welcomed in. For traditions that don't stay up this late and don't offer a service on Christmas Day, a Christmas Eve service may function more as the opening celebration of Christmas. If this is the case in your context, you may want to look ahead in the next chapter to the lectionary texts prescribed for Christmas Day. The lectionary offers three sets of texts for the first day of the season of Christmas, which could be beneficial in planning a Christmas Eve service that welcomes in the Christmas season.

In the season of Advent, we are taught to anticipate God's activity. We are taught to wait well. This often requires us to slow down so we can know what we're actually waiting for and learn to hope like Isaiah (see Isa. 64:1–9); to stop talking so we can hear what others are saying and learn to listen like Zechariah (see Luke 1:8–20); and to surrender what control we think we have and learn to trust like Mary (see Luke 1:26–38). When your corporate worship services are built to practice these habits of Advent, don't be surprised when you begin to see Christ come in the lives of your people.

# CHRISTMAS

## The Invitation to Celebrate Christ's Presence on Earth

### TIME

12 days

*December 25 through January 5*

### COLOR

White with gold accent

*(color of joy and celebration)*

### SPECIAL DAYS

- **Christmas Day** (December 25, the first day of the season of Christmas)
- The **Feast of the Holy Innocents** (December 28)
- The **Feast of the Holy Name of Jesus** (January 1)

I apologize beforehand for what I'm about to make your brain do, but do you recall the song "The Twelve Days of Christmas"? Though it might still hold the record for the most annoying Christmas song (and you may catch yourself humming it for the next hour or so), it is correct in teaching that there are in fact twelve days in the season of Christmas. And no, the season does not start the day after Halloween, as most department stores assume. The season begins on December 25 and lasts through January 5.

God has been born in the flesh. Our Creator is among us. He is fragile, dependent, hungry, speechless, humbled. We don't entirely understand what is happening yet—it is a mystery—but we do know that God has seen us, and he has acted by stepping into our reality. Our God is a personal God, a God with a mom and a dad, with friends, with likes and dislikes. He is a God that falls down and bruises his knees and at times really has to go to the bathroom. And though we can't understand all that will eventually unfold after he enters the world, in this season we remember that God is with us. Therefore, it is a season of celebration.

| | YEAR A | B | C |
|---|---|---|---|
| | *Nativity of the Lord I* | | |
| **CHRISTMAS DAY** *December 25* (*or Christmas Eve*) | Isaiah 9:2–7<br>Psalm 96<br>Titus 2:11–14<br>Luke 2:1–14 (15–20) | | |
| | *Nativity of the Lord II* | | |
| | Isaiah 62:6–12<br>Psalm 97<br>Titus 3:4–7<br>Luke 2:(1–7) 8–20 | | |
| | *Nativity of the Lord III* | | |
| | Isaiah 52:7–10<br>Psalm 98<br>Hebrews 1:1–4 (5–12)<br>John 1:1–14 | | |
| **WEEK 1** | Isaiah 63:7–9<br>Psalm 148<br>Hebrews 2:10-18<br>Matthew 2:13-23 | | |
| **FEAST OF THE HOLY NAME OF JESUS** *January 1* | Numbers 6:22–27<br>Psalm 8<br>Galatians 4:4–7<br>*or* Philippians 2:5–11<br>Luke 2:15–21 | | |
| **WEEK 2** | Jeremiah 31:7–14<br>Psalm 147:12-20<br>Ephesians 1:3–14<br>John 1:(1-9) 10-18 | | |

White, the color of the season of Christmas, is a color of joy and celebration and matches the praise offered throughout the prophecies, psalms, epistles, and Gospel readings of the assigned lectionary texts. **Christmas Day** (December 25) is set apart as a special day within the season, as is January 1, celebrated in some denominations as the **Feast of the Holy Name of Jesus**. This day is the eighth day of the season, the day Jesus would have been circumcised and received his name by Jewish tradition (see Luke 2:21).[1] However, in the Aaronic blessing that is prescribed in the lectionary for this day, we also celebrate God giving *us* his name as well:

> The Lord spoke to Moses: Tell Aaron and his sons: You will bless the Israelites as follows. Say to them:
>
> The Lord bless you and protect you.
> The Lord make his face shine on you and be gracious to you.
> The Lord lift up his face to you and grant you peace.
>
> They will place my name on the Israelites, and I will bless them.
>
> —Numbers 6:22–27 (CEB)

A far less commemorated special day within the season of Christmas is the **Feast of the Holy Innocents** or **Childermas** (commemorated by the Western tradition on December 28 and Eastern tradition on December 29). On this day, the church mournfully remembers Herod's massacre of young male children in Bethlehem, two years old and younger, in his attempt to remove the threat of this "newborn king of the Jews" (see Matt. 2:1–18). You may have heard the melody of the sixteenth-century English "Coventry Carol." Often this song will only be played instrumentally as the words aren't the most festive. Verse three reads:

> Herod the king, in his raging,
> Charged he hath this day
> His men of might in his own sight,
> All children young to slay.[2]

This day is certainly a sharp turn within the season. Infanticide is a sobering, dark reality right after Light himself enters the world. It reminds us that beyond this early celebration in the Christian Year, there is a long and difficult journey looming ahead. Christ has entered the world, and now we look to him to save the world. God is not surprised by the horrific response of humanity to his coming; in fact, some might consider Herod's response a foretelling of what is to come. This was one battle, but the triumph of the war is still to be determined.

## WAYS TO JOIN THE CELEBRATION OF CHRISTMAS

### CHRISTMAS SONGS

If you have sought to save Christmas songs until the season began, now is the time to let out all the stops. It's a celebration, so sing Christmas songs that your people know. (Now is not the time to teach new songs.) And sing these songs each Sunday in the season, not just the first (though, depending on how the days fall in a particular year, the season might only have one Sunday). Because the season is so short and there are so many great Christmas carols your congregation and visitors will know, consider ways to incorporate songs within other elements as well. Consider this Scripture passage from Luke 2:8–20 being read by three readers and band members with the verses of "The First Noel" being sung as a refrain.

Reader 1: That night there were shepherds staying in the fields nearby, keeping watch over their flocks by night. Suddenly, an angel of the Lord appeared to them, and the glory of the Lord surrounded them. They were terrified, but the angel said to them: "Do not be afraid. I bring you good news of great joy that will be for all the people."

***All:*** ***The first Noel, the angel did say,***
***was to certain poor shepherd in fields as they lay—***
***in fields where they lay keeping their sheep***
***on a cold winter's night that was so deep.***
***Noel, noel, noel, noel! Born is the King of Israel!***

Reader 2: The Savior has been born today in Bethlehem, the city of David! And you will recognize him by this sign: You will find a baby wrapped snugly in strips of cloth, lying in a manger.

Suddenly, the angel was joined by a vast host of others—the armies of heaven—praising God and saying,

*Band:* *Glory to God in highest heaven,*
*and peace on earth to people he favors.*

Reader 2: When the angels had returned to heaven, the shepherds said to each other, "Let's go to Bethlehem! Let's see this thing that has happened, which the Lord has told us about."

***All:*** ***They looked up and saw a star***
***shining in the East beyond them far***
***and to the earth it gave great light***
***and so it continued both day and night.***
***Noel, noel, noel, noel! Born is the King of Israel!***

Reader 3: They hurried to the village and found Mary and Joseph. And there was the baby, lying in the manger. After seeing him, the shepherds told everyone what had happened and what the angel had said to them about this child. All who heard the shepherds' story were astonished, but Mary kept all these things in her heart and thought about them often. The shepherds went back to their flocks, glorifying and praising God for all they had heard and seen. It was just as the angel had told them.

*All:* ***Then let us all with one accord***
***sing praises to our heavenly Lord***
***that hath made heav'n and earth of nought***
***and with his blood mankind has bought.***
***Noel, noel, noel, noel! Born is the King of Israel!***[3]

## THE FEAST OF THE HOLY NAME OF JESUS SUNDAY

The Sunday closest to January 1 is often given to themes of new beginnings and resolutions for the new year. Though this approach is certainly contextual to the social calendar, commemorating the Feast of the Holy Name of Jesus bases our new beginnings in the life of Christ. On this day, we move beyond celebrating just Christ's presence to celebrating his participation in our human activities. Just as Christ enters the world as a Jew and submits himself to the traditions of the Jewish community (e.g., circumcision), we are invited to ask if there are ways we could humble ourselves more to the communities in which Christ has placed us. Do we bear an identity from the community we are a part of? Have we been marked by it? Or are we detached—standing at a distance?

Psalm 8 is ascribed to this day and the psalmist both humbles and edifies us:

> O LORD, our Lord, your majestic name fills the earth!
> Your glory is higher than the heavens. . . .
> What are mere mortals that you should think about them,
> human beings that you should care for them?
> Yet you made them only a little lower than God
> And crowned them with glory and honor.
> You gave them charge of everything you made,
> putting all things under their authority.
>
> —Psalm 8:1, 4–6

The psalmist reveals God's care for us but reminds us that he has called us to take care of everything he made. Through Jesus, God reveals that the first step in this guardianship is humility. He came as a weak, frail baby. The Feast of the Holy Name of Jesus reminds us that if we are to care for the world, we must model Christ, who stepped into our world, taking a human name and a human mark, revealing divinity through humanity.

This is a great Sunday to schedule baptisms, bearing witness to the act of a person submitting themselves to their community of believers. They come out of the water with a new name, marked by a new identity. Perhaps your congregation needs to hear about someone that humbled themselves to a community they were called to. Perhaps you could offer a commissioning time within the service to send everyone in your congregation out to their jobs, schools, or homes in the name of Jesus. You could even use the Aaronic blessing from the Old Testament lesson assigned to the day.

Don't get me wrong; it's always great to reevaluate our habits. But what if we didn't reevaluate them just because it's a new year or because we want to look better in the mirror? What if, instead, we reevaluated them as a response to the manifestation of God in human form? For he was "born through a woman, and born under the Law . . . so that we could be adopted. . . . Therefore, you are no longer a slave but a son or daughter, and if you are his child, then you are also an heir through God" (Gal. 4:4–7 CEB). We share an identity with Life himself; therefore, we make healthy choices not for vanity's sake, but because Christ *is* life, and we know him more and reveal him more when we choose life-giving habits.

## THE FEAST OF THE HOLY INNOCENTS

If the Feast of the Holy Innocents happened to fall on a Sunday, perhaps during a pastoral prayer ("Prayers of the People"), the leader could mention those sometimes referred to as the first martyrs of the church and join the cry of the parents in Bethlehem by adding our own laments of brokenness. Perhaps pause could be given to allow people to add their own laments, and meanwhile the "Coventry Carol" could be hummed or played by an instrument during these pauses. This would allow those whose own life circumstances don't currently match the Christmas season to feel that, even amidst celebration, God hears our pain. The prayer could end with the pastor calling God to act on our behalf, just as he did in being Emmanuel, God with us. We need him to act in these situations and make his presence known. Then perhaps the congregation could join together in singing a song that restates God's presence with us.

## NATIVITY ART

Next to the cross, the nativity is probably one of the most commonly depicted scenes within Christian fine art. The beauty of this commonality is the diversity of these depictions. There are culturally specific nativity scenes that push our brains to see a perspective broader than what we grew up seeing. In my context, we make an effort to use artist depictions that are either more closely related to the actual culture of Christ, or that simply embrace the perspective of another culture. Perhaps a picture could be presented during a Scripture reading, a prelude, or a special song. If your church has a social media presence, perhaps twelve different cultures' depictions of the nativity could be shared each day of the Christmas season.

## TWELVE-DAY CALENDAR

Since I work in an evangelical context that is still fairly unfamiliar with all the details of the Christian Year, it requires a lot of intentionality to invite the congregation to explore what it might look like to celebrate Christmas as a season rather than just one day. I would argue that Christmas is the most difficult season to do anything with because of how short it is. Some years there is only one Sunday in the entire season. This brings up an important point: the Christian Year is not 52 days long (Sundays in a year), it is 365 days long. In this resource, I am focusing primarily on those times the body of believers gather together for corporate worship (upper case *L*iturgy). However, of all the seasons, the season of Christmas requires "homework" (lower case *l*iturgy) if our congregations are going to be formed by these twelve days of celebration.

Upon reading this, a child might declare, "Twelve days of presents!" Which, if your family regularly gives gifts on the first day of Christmas, perhaps they have a good point. I'd just suggest spreading out the gifts over the twelve days rather than multiplying the number of gifts by twelve *(and all the kids let out a groan of despair)*. Perhaps a tradition that would be more in line with the lessons of the Feast of the Holy Name of Jesus would be that after your family shares gifts on the first day of Christmas, your family might then find eleven other families or persons to bless throughout the remainder of the season—each day sharing cookies, dinner, or gifts with others.

In an attempt to encourage our congregation to celebrate the full season of Christmas, one of our team members took the lead on providing small twelve-day calendars for families or communities of friends to take home on Christmas Eve and journey through the season together. Each day of the calendar offered a Scripture reading for the family or community to read together and an activity to encourage them to be intentional with the season, as well as to savor the celebration. The first eight days sought to cultivate celebration within the family or community, while the last four days (the days following the Feast of the Holy Name of Jesus) invited the family or community to serve those outside their community. Below you'll find a list of the twelve activities we suggested:

***Day 1:*** Open and enjoy any gifts you were given.

***Day 2:*** Watch a Christmas movie with your family or friends.

***Day 3:*** Take a nap, or sleep in. Rest.

***Day 4:*** Go ice skating, sledding, or have a snowball fight with friends or family.

***Day 5:*** Enjoy or play some Christmas music—maybe even go Christmas caroling.

***Day 6:*** Read a good book with a nice Christmas drink.

***Day 7:*** Eat a meal with family or friends and celebrate New Year's Eve together.

***Day 8:*** Bring order to some area in your home—clean a room, do the dishes, etc.

***Day 9:*** Bake Christmas treats together.

***Day 10:*** Pay for someone else's coffee.

***Day 11:*** Write and send a Christmas card.

***Day 12:*** Give a final Christmas present to someone else.

Some might consider their Christmas Eve service to be a Christmas special service. As mentioned in the previous chapter, some churches even hold their service so late they actually welcome in Christmas morning at midnight. Beyond this, the season of Christmas is so short I would suggest not offering any other special service in this season. Your congregation, if they aren't away visiting family, probably have enough school, community, and work events that recruiting volunteers for a special service in this season may add more stress than celebration to everyone's life. I suggest you encourage your congregation to be with people in this season. As Christ came to be among us, may we be among others. Of any season to be outside the church walls, Christmas pushes us to "Go, tell it on the mountain, that Jesus Christ is born!"

# EPIPHANY

## The Invitation to Wonder at Christ's Work on Earth

---

### TIME

Begins on January 6
*through the start of Lent*
*(Ash Wednesday)*

### COLOR

Green
*(color of growth)*

### SPECIAL DAYS

- The **Epiphany** (January 6, the first day of the season of Epiphany)
- **Transfiguration Sunday** (the Sunday before Ash Wednesday)
  *Color changes to white (color of joy and celebration)*

---

In all the conversations I have about the Christian Year, it seems that Epiphany ties with Ordinary Time for the least understood season. It doesn't help that the word *Epiphany* is used infrequently. If you've heard it in a sentence, it was probably something like: "On my way home from work, I had an epiphany." It is that moment the lightbulb goes off in your head and you have a great idea. So, what's the *season* of Epiphany? Is it a season of a bunch of lightbulb moments? Well, in a sense, yes.

Throughout the season of Epiphany, we remember moments when it hits us (like a lightbulb going off), "Wait a moment: Jesus—this human—is God!" We recount stories about Jesus: the magi visiting him, his baptism, when he turns water into wine, calling his first disciples, his temptation in the desert, his sermons, as well as many other miracles, culminating at his transfiguration. God is standing with his people in the flesh; God has become human. What does this mean—for God and for humanity? What's going to happen next? What's God going to do as he walks upon the earth? Through these epiphanies, we stand in awe and wonder, and join the disciples in the only thing left to do: leave everything and follow him.

Epiphany, similar to Ordinary Time, doesn't have a set number of weeks. The green seasons of growth (Epiphany and Ordinary Time) are like vines that fill as much space as they've been given. Epiphany fills the space of ***the* Epiphany** (January 6) until the start of Lent on Ash Wednesday. This means that some years Epiphany will only be four weeks, while other years the season could be up to nine weeks. No matter how long the season is, the last Sunday of the season (the Sunday before Ash Wednesday) is called **Transfiguration Sunday**.

| | YEAR A | YEAR B | YEAR C |
|---|---|---|---|
| **THE EPIPHANY** *January 6* | Isaiah 60:1–6<br>Psalm 72:1–7, 10–14<br>Ephesians 3:1–12<br>Matthew 2:1–12 | | |
| **WEEK 1** | Isaiah 42:1–9<br>Psalm 29<br>Acts 10:34–43<br>Matthew 3:13–17 | Genesis 1:1–5<br>Psalm 29<br>Acts 19:1–7<br>Mark 1:4–11 | Isaiah 43:1–7<br>Psalm 29<br>Acts 8:14–17<br>Luke 3:15–17, 21–22 |
| **WEEK 2** | Isaiah 49:1–7<br>Psalm 40:1–11<br>1 Corinthians 1:1–9<br>John 1:29–42 | 1 Samuel 3:1–10 (11–20)<br>Psalm 139:1–6, 13–18<br>1 Corinthians 6:12–20<br>John 1:43–51 | Isaiah 62:1–5<br>Psalm 36:5–10<br>1 Corinthians 12:1–11<br>John 2:1–11 |
| **WEEK 3** | Isaiah 9:1–4<br>Psalm 27:1, 4–9<br>1 Corinthians 1:10–18<br>Matthew 4:12–23 | Jonah 3:1–5, 10<br>Psalm 62:5–12<br>1 Corinthians 7:29–31<br>Mark 1:14–20 | Nehemiah 8:1–3, 5–6, 8–10<br>Psalm 19<br>1 Corinthians 12:12–31a<br>Luke 4:14–21 |
| **WEEK 4** | Micah 6:1–8<br>Psalm 15<br>1 Corinthians 1:18–31<br>Matthew 5:1–12 | Deuteronomy 18:15–20<br>Psalm 111<br>1 Corinthians 8:1–13<br>Mark 1:21–28 | Jeremiah 1:4–10<br>Psalm 71:1–6<br>1 Corinthians 13:1–13<br>Luke 4:21–30 |
| **WEEK 5** | Isaiah 58:1–9a (9b–12)<br>Psalm 112:1–9(10)<br>1 Corinthians 2:1–12 (13–16)<br>Matthew 5:13–20 | Isaiah 40:21–31<br>Psalm 147:1–11, 20c<br>1 Corinthians 9:16–23<br>Mark 1:29–39 | Isaiah 6:1–8 (9–13)<br>Psalm 138<br>1 Corinthians 15:1–11<br>Luke 5:1–11 |
| **WEEK 6** | Deuteronomy 30:15–20<br>Psalm 119:1–8<br>1 Corinthians 3:1–9<br>Matthew 5:21–37 | 2 Kings 5:1–14<br>Psalm 30<br>1 Corinthians 9:24–27<br>Mark 1:40–45 | Jeremiah 17:5–10<br>Psalm 1<br>1 Corinthians 15:12–20<br>Luke 6:17–26 |
| **WEEK 7** | Leviticus 19:1–2, 9–18<br>Psalm 119:33–40<br>1 Corinthians 3:10–11, 16–23<br>Matthew 5:38–48 | Isaiah 43:18–25<br>Psalm 41<br>2 Corinthians 1:18–22<br>Mark 2:1–12 | Genesis 45:3–11, 15<br>Psalm 37:1–11, 39–40<br>1 Corinthians 15:35–38, 42–50<br>Luke 6:27–38 |

| | YEAR A | YEAR B | YEAR C |
|---|---|---|---|
| **WEEK 8** | Isaiah 49:8–16a<br>Psalm 131<br>1 Corinthians 4:1–5<br>Matthew 6:24–34 | Hosea 2:14–20<br>Psalm 103:1–13, 22<br>2 Corinthians 3:1–6<br>Mark 2:13–22 | Isaiah 55:10–13<br>Psalm 92:1–4, 12–15<br>1 Corinthians 15:51–58<br>Luke 6:39–49 |
| **TRANSFIGURATION SUNDAY** *(The Sunday before Ash Wednesday)* | | | |
| | Exodus 24:12–18<br>Psalm 2 *or* 99<br>2 Peter 1:16–21<br>Matthew 17:1–9 | 2 Kings 2:1–12<br>Psalm 50:1–6<br>2 Corinthians 4:3–6<br>Mark 9:2–9 | Exodus 34:29–35<br>Psalm 99<br>2 Corinthians 3:12—4:2<br>Luke 9:28–36 (37–43a) |

Epiphany is a *wonder-full* season culminating in the revelation of Christ in all his glory atop a mountain. Not only do we witness the appearance of Elijah and Moses (finally making it to the promised land, I might add), but we hear a voice from a cloud say about Jesus, "This is my dearly loved Son. Listen to him" (Mark 9:7). The statement echoes the voice from heaven heard at Jesus' baptism (read on the first week of the season), "You are my dearly loved Son, and you bring me great joy" (Mark 1:11). Mark and Luke are the only two Gospel writers that record the difference in point of view. At his baptism the Father talks to Jesus, "*You* are my dearly loved Son," but at the transfiguration, the Father turns to us and says, "*This* is my dearly loved Son. Listen to *him*!"

Throughout the season of Epiphany, we are privy to witnessing the activity of Christ and are called to join the Father's declaration of the Son, "Yes, you are the Son of God!" But in this final scene, when we experience our friend and teacher being transformed and his clothes becoming dazzling white, "far whiter than any earthly bleach could ever make them" (Mark 9:3), there is no longer any doubt. And we blurt out, like Peter, "Rabbi, it's *wonderful* for us to be here! Let's make three shelters as memorials—one for you, one for Moses, and one for Elijah" (v. 5, emphasis added). I appreciate Mark's inclusion of what was really happening here, almost like a confession: "[Peter] said this because he didn't really know what else to say, for they were all terrified" (v. 6). Peter knew he was witnessing holy things, and he was searching for some way to respond to this great revelation. However, it would be the Father himself that gave instruction on how we ought to respond to this revelation of Christ: "This is my dearly loved Son," he said. "*Listen to him*" (v. 7, emphasis added).

## WAYS TO JOIN THE WONDER OF EPIPHANY

### TELL THE STORIES

Many of the lectionary texts for the season of Epiphany give us the opportunity to listen to Jesus' teachings. However, not only do we get to hear what he *says*, but we get to see what he *did*. The primary way to join in the wonder of the season is to remember the stories of God with us—on this earth—revealing a reality that our eyes had not yet seen and our ears had not yet heard. But we pray that throughout this season we might hear Christ say to us as he did to his disciples, "Blessed are your eyes, because they see; and your ears, because they hear" (Matt. 13:16). So, reenact the stories of Christ so we may hear *and* see them. Tell the stories of his interaction with the crowds, preach from his sermons, act out his parables using people of all ages as characters. Bow with the magi, remember your own baptism into Christ, taste transformed wine, and experience a similar transformation as your congregation witnesses Christ's ministry unfold.

There are numerous ways to tell stories. Basic readers can stretch themselves by researching the field of oral interpretation of literature. You could break a story into a couple different scenes and use the art of tableau: frozen characters creating a specific scene—like a children's book with illustrations. Split the reading up between readers, give lines to the congregation, use a prop or two that is either mentioned in the text or could symbolize something within the text. Write musical underscores to capture the ethos of the text. Memorize and recite these stories, enacting Jesus' words *then* to your congregation *today*. Let the talents already within your context give birth to creative ways to wonder at these stories of Christ.

A favorite storytelling technique in my context, particularly for the stories of Epiphany, is creating "Kids' Scripture Videos," as we call them. Get a group of kids, some old bedsheets and bathrobes to capture some early 30s Jewish looks, maybe some fake beards, and have the kids act out these miraculous stories of Christ. Nowadays, smartphones take video footage of high enough quality that you don't need other expensive video equipment. Use a free movie-making app to edit the scenes. Take out the audio and add in a recording of the kids reading their assigned characters. Look online and you'll find a lot of examples to inspire creativity for your own context.[1]

Another medium you could use to remember these stories of Christ is fine art. There are numerous pieces that have already been created that portray Christ's miracles, but these stories also act as great prompts if you were to ask some members of your congregation to depict them. Hang them in an "art gallery" in a church hallway, use them as bulletin covers, or display them on the screen during the Scripture reading. These stories include a lot of characters, a lot of objects or props, and a lot of expression. In a way, by reenacting these stories—whether in fine art, media, or with the oral interpretation of literature—you and your congregation will find yourselves amongst the crowd that first witnessed Christ. We see him and we hear him through the presentation of his Word.

## REMEMBER YOUR BAPTISM

As mentioned earlier in this chapter, the texts assigned to the first Sunday of Epiphany recount the baptism of our Lord in the Jordan River. Though this is another great opportunity to schedule baptisms for your context—if you didn't do so already on the Feast of the Holy Name of Jesus during Christmas—you might also invite your people to remember their own baptisms. Place a basin, or font, of water from the baptismal pool either at the front of the nave for your people to come forward during a specific element of the service, or at the exits for people as they are sent out. This practice might be foreign to many evangelicals and might evoke their aversion to anything that appears ritualistic. However, if it is explained well and offered as an invitation to remember that God's grace is still at work in their lives, perhaps your congregation might find this act sacred. Such an invitation could be as follows:

> Just as we remembered Christ's baptism in the Jordan River, many of us in this room can remember our own baptisms into his life. And though we are only baptized once, we are called to live a life of baptism every day—living a life that reveals the grace we have received. Today, as you leave, you'll notice that there are small basins (or fonts) of water at the doors. This may seem foreign to some of you, but it can serve a very sacred purpose. If you've been baptized, we invite you to simply dip a finger in the water—maybe you even want to touch your forehead to feel the cleansing water all the more. May this water remind you of your baptism, your call to live in that baptism, and that God's grace is still at work in your life.

## TRANSFIGURATION SUNDAY

As mentioned in the introduction of this season, Transfiguration Sunday is the final Sunday of Epiphany. A common method for remembering this story in my context is through the use of symbol and tableau. Traditionally, a white cloth is placed on the altar on this special Sunday even though the color of the season is green. However, in my context, we often don't introduce this cloth until the presentation of the Word, usually during the reenactment of the transfiguration scene. See below the script based on Mark 9:2–9, which is read by a narrator, as well as tableau scenes to accompany the text. The start of each new scene would be indicated by sounding a drum, clave, or bell.

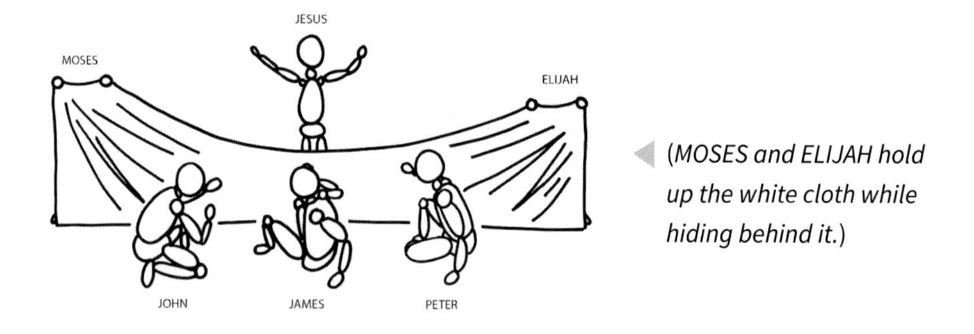


*(MOSES and ELIJAH hold up the white cloth while hiding behind it.)*

Reader: Jesus took Peter, James, and John, and led them up a high mountain to be alone. As the men watched, Jesus' appearance was transformed, and his clothes became dazzling white, far whiter than any earthly bleach could ever make them.

*(MOSES and ELIJAH show their faces.)*

Then Elijah and Moses appeared and began talking with Jesus.

Peter exclaimed, "Rabbi, it's wonderful for us to be here! Let's make three shelters as memorials—one for you, one for Moses, and one for Elijah." He said this because he didn't really know what else to say, for they were all terrified.

*(MOSES and ELIJAH violently shake the cloth over the disciples during the next reading.)*

Then a cloud overshadowed them, and a voice from the cloud said, "This is my dearly loved Son. Listen to him."

*(MOSES and ELIJAH quickly place the white cloth on the altar and "disappear" from the room.)*

Suddenly, when they looked around, Moses and Elijah were gone, and they saw only Jesus with them. As they went back down the mountain, he told them not to tell anyone what they had seen until the Son of Man had risen from the dead.

This is where the text ends in both Year A (which uses Matthew's Gospel) and Year B (which uses Mark's Gospel). However, in Year C (when Luke is assigned), the lectionary offers an additional narrative following the transfiguration: Jesus' healing of a demon-possessed boy. Both Matthew and Mark include this story in their Gospels but only in Year C is it an optional inclusion on Transfiguration Sunday. If you include this narrative, you might consider how you might still incorporate the white cloth in this scene. Perhaps when Jesus heals the boy, he pulls the cloth from the altar and dresses the boy in it. Through this, we witness the same glory of Christ revealed on the mountain in the exorcising of a demon that made a boy "unable to hear and speak" (Mark 9:25), a detail that Matthew and Luke both leave out.

I do not know why the organizers of the lectionary decided not to include this portion of the story each year, and why it is Luke's version they choose to include when they do (and only as an option), but I'm not writing here a critique of the lectionary. I think the inclusion of the story—even if not every year and no matter if from Matthew, Mark, or Luke—is a beneficial juxtaposition to the transfiguration narrative. The voice told the disciples, in essence, "Don't build a shelter. Don't build a memorial. Listen to my Son" (Mark 9:5–7). Then, upon walking down from this mountaintop worship experience, the disciples witness Jesus rebuke a spirit, saying, "Listen, you spirit that makes this boy unable to hear and to speak . . . I command you to come out of this child and never enter him again!" (v. 25).

Oh Christ, dearly loved Son of God, if there is any evil in us that makes us unable to hear and to speak, rebuke it so that—whether on the mountain top or among the crowd—we may listen to your voice and proclaim your praise. Amen.

## SPECIAL SERVICES

January 6, the first day of the season of Epiphany and *the* Epiphany of the Lord, commemorates the magi's visit to the Christ child. Because the date never changes, the start of the season is rarely on a Sunday. Therefore, you could offer an Epiphany special service on **January 6** that frames the season for your people, or you could use this story as a call to worship on the first Sunday after the season of Christmas. We are invited to join the magi in worshiping our King and offering him gifts of praise. Beyond this, there aren't special services common to Epiphany, probably because of the diverse perspectives of the season as a whole.

Some traditions will celebrate *the* Epiphany, but consider the weeks following to simply be a portion of Ordinary Time, not adhering to an actual season of Epiphany. As I wrote in the introduction of this book, I am not offering a historical overview of the Christian Year, I am only offering suggestions to your local context on how to make the life of Christ a part of your corporate identity. Obviously, from the inclusion of this chapter, I think Epiphany as a season is a beautiful movement to the sonata of Christ's life. And, if you're looking to include a special service, there's plenty of content from this portion of Christ's life to build a service out of. However, in recognizing that you probably just offered a Christmas Eve service and are already thinking about an Ash Wednesday service, it might be wise to let Epiphany be a season absent of services outside of the Sunday service. I could also argue that, similar to the season of Christmas, an absence of special services might be fitting for this season as well. Let me explain:

In Epiphany, we witness the teachings of Christ and the work of Christ. I might suggest that in a season that is full of wonder at the manifestation of God with us—the divine sharing himself with humanity in *our* context—the best special service a church could offer in this season, is just that: special *service* to those outside the body of believers. The Greek word for worship is *leitourgia*, where we get our English word *liturgy*. It literally means "the work of the people." The word may seem archaic and it might conjure up images of a book of corporate readings or even a particular style of doing church. But, simply put, liturgy is everything we do in corporate worship—every church has a liturgy. But our liturgy is not confined inside the church walls. When we love our neighbor, this is our liturgy—our worship. Just as when we pray to God, offer our tithes, hear a sermon, or yes, sing a song, it is all our worship—our liturgy—the work of God's people responding to his revelation.

David Stubbs shares a phrase touted by the Eastern Orthodox: "the liturgy after the Liturgy."[2] What happens on Sunday is just the beginning of our worship (a blueprint of how things should be). Monday through Saturday is our worship after our Worship. In a sense, God is revealed to us in and through the corporate gathering of believers (like Christ transfigured on a mountaintop) and we respond by the way we live our life afterward (like Christ transfiguring lives among the crowd). So, instead of a special evening service in this season, I challenge you to organize ways for your congregation to serve your community. If you have small groups, encourage your leaders to use one of their meeting times to go serve as a team somewhere. Come down the mountain after seeing the glory of Christ and enter the crowd, listening for Jesus' direction. You might just see Christ still at work and wonder at his presence anew.

# LENT

## The Invitation to Reckon Our Life with Christ's Life and Death

### TIME

6 weeks
*beginning on Ash Wednesday continuing until the start of Easter*

### COLOR

Purple
*(color of penitence and royalty)*

### SPECIAL DAYS

- **Ash Wednesday** (the Sunday after Transfiguration Sunday)
- **Holy Week** (the final week before Easter)

*Color changes to red (color of blood, passion, and love)*

Palm Sunday
Holy Monday
Holy Tuesday
Holy Wednesday
Holy Thursday (sometimes called Maundy Thursday)

*Color changes to black (color of death)*

Good Friday
Holy Saturday

Every good story reaches a point when life seems too good to be true, and usually it is. The audience gets a hint that something bad is about to happen. There is conflict, tension, hidden layers that begin to unfold. Things aren't what they seemed to be. The season of Lent is this shift in the story of Christ's life.

The primary antagonist is introduced as Jesus is led into the wilderness and tempted by the devil. Sides begin to be formed between Christ's followers and the religious leaders. Jesus even tells his disciples of his looming suffering and death. The tension is palpable as Peter reprimands him for saying such things. This isn't the story Jesus' followers had in mind. The plan Jesus was laying out was a plan of defeat, not victory. Just a couple days before the season of Lent we saw Jesus, in all his glory, transfigured with Elijah and Moses and then, right after, heal a demon-possessed boy. "Listen to him," the Father told us. But that was then, and this is now. Jesus isn't acting like we thought he would as he resolutely sets out for Jerusalem, knowing full well what doom lies ahead.

The primary color for this season is purple, a color of penitence and royalty. Even the color chosen to symbolize the season holds within it a tension: an affirmation of Christ as king and the sorrow for the crown of thorns he will soon wear. In this season, the people of God journey with Christ as he embraces the fullness of his humanity—even the humanness of death. We are called to reckon with our own humanness in Lent, that from dust we came and to dust we shall return. This is a season when we are challenged to stop pretending. We are invited to confess, to reckon with our pain, fear, and inability to fix all that is broken in the world. We *have been* broken, we *have done* the breaking, and Christ will be broken for all.

In an **Ash Wednesday** sermon a couple years ago, I likened the season of Lent to the period in which one's broken bone is healed. Though many emotions can surround how a bone was broken—whether it was an accident of our own, the result of someone else's recklessness, or intentional evil done to us—the first step is to admit that the bone is broken. If we don't begin there, pretending instead that we are fine, the bone will calcify and become a permanent distortion, leaving us to live a life as less than who we could be. After admitting our brokenness, we must get the bone set, receive a cast to keep it in place, and begin a journey of restoration.

On the first day of the season of Lent, it is fitting to gather as a corporate body and, after confessing our brokenness, come to the altar (to be "set") and receive a sign of the cross in ash on our forehead (the symbol of our "cast"). We are challenged to ask God what things we should give up or take on in this season to best cooperate with his healing rhythm in our life, just as a patient is given exercises and restrictions, not to accomplish the healing, but rather to promote the best environment for healing. Then, after "forty days," perhaps we can take the cast off.[1]

Throughout Lent we journey with Christ—casts and all—to the cross, embracing what he told his disciples: "If any of you wants to be my follower, you must give up your own way, take up your cross daily, and follow me. If you try to hang on to your life, you will lose it. But if you give up your life for my sake, you will save it" (Luke 9:23–24). We watch as the Creator of the universe gets trampled by his own creation. He never says a mumbling word, subjecting himself to death, even death on a cross. Like Christ, we are invited to look beyond our reality—the bad and the good—and give our lives to something greater than ourselves. As we journey with him, we are reckoned with the limitations of our humanness and left waiting for an answer bigger than ourselves. Though this journey seems like dying, we have no choice but to trust the way of Jesus.

| | YEAR A | YEAR B | YEAR C |
|---|---|---|---|
| ASH WEDNESDAY | Joel 2:1–2, 12–17<br>*or* Isaiah 58:1–12<br>Psalm 51:1–17<br>2 Corinthians 5:20b—6:10<br>Matthew 6:1–6, 16–21 | | |
| WEEK 1 | Genesis 2:15–17; 3:1–7<br>Psalm 32<br>Romans 5:12–19<br>Matthew 4:1–11 | Genesis 9:8–17<br>Psalm 25:1–10<br>1 Peter 3:18–22<br>Mark 1:9–15 | Deuteronomy 26:1–11<br>Psalm 91:1–2, 9–16<br>Romans 10:8b–13<br>Luke 4:1–13 |
| WEEK 2 | Genesis 12:1–4a<br>Psalm 121<br>Romans 4:1–5, 13–17<br>John 3:1–17<br>*or* Matthew 17:1-9 | Genesis 17:1–7, 15–16<br>Psalm 22:23–31<br>Romans 4:13–25<br>Mark 8:31–38<br>*or* 9:2–9 | Genesis 15:1–12, 17–18<br>Psalm 27<br>Philippians 3:17—4:1<br>Luke 13:31–35<br>*or* 9:28-36 (37-43a) |
| WEEK 3 | Exodus 17:1–7<br>Psalm 95<br>Romans 5:1–11<br>John 4:5–42 | Exodus 20:1–17<br>Psalm 19<br>1 Corinthians 1:18–25<br>John 2:13–22 | Isaiah 55:1–9<br>Psalm 63:1–8<br>1 Corinthians 10:1–13<br>Luke 13:1–9 |
| WEEK 4 | 1 Samuel 16:1–13<br>Psalm 23<br>Ephesians 5:8–14<br>John 9:1–41 | Numbers 21:4–9<br>Psalm 107:1–3, 17–22<br>Ephesians 2:1–10<br>John 3:14–21 | Joshua 5:9–12<br>Psalm 32<br>2 Corinthians 5:16–21<br>Luke 15:1–3, 11b–32 |
| WEEK 5 | Ezekiel 37:1–14<br>Psalm 130<br>Romans 8:6–11<br>John 11:1–45 | Jeremiah 31:31–34<br>Psalm 51:1–12<br>*or* 119:9–16<br>Hebrews 5:5–10<br>John 12:20–33 | Isaiah 43:16–21<br>Psalm 126<br>Philippians 3:4b–14<br>John 12:1–8 |

## HOLY WEEK

| | | | |
|---|---|---|---|
| **WEEK 6**<br>*Palm Sunday* | *Texts for the Palms*<br>Matthew 21:1–11<br>Psalm 118:1–2, 19–29 | *Texts for the Palms*<br>Mark 11:1–11<br>*or* John 12:12–16<br>Psalm 118:1–2, 19–29 | *Texts for the Palms*<br>Luke 19:28–40<br>Psalm 118:1–2, 19–29 |
| | Isaiah 50:4–9a<br>Psalm 31:9–16<br>Philippians 2:5–11<br>Matthew 26:14—27:66<br>*or* 27:11–54 | Isaiah 50:4–9a<br>Psalm 31:9–16<br>Philippians 2:5–11<br>Mark 14:1—15:47<br>*or* 15:1–39 (40–47) | Isaiah 50:4–9a<br>Psalm 31:9–16<br>Philippians 2:5–11<br>Luke 22:14—23:56<br>*or* 23:1–49 |

| | |
|---|---|
| **HOLY MONDAY** | Isaiah 42:1–9<br>Psalm 36:5–11<br>Hebrews 9:11–15<br>John 12:1–11 |
| **HOLY TUESDAY** | Isaiah 49:1–7<br>Psalm 71:1–14<br>1 Corinthians 1:18–31<br>John 12:20–36 |
| **HOLY WEDNESDAY** | Isaiah 50:4–9a<br>Psalm 70<br>Hebrews 12:1–3<br>John 13:21–32 |
| **HOLY (MAUNDY) THURSDAY** | Exodus 12:1–4 (5–10), 11–14<br>Psalm 116:1–2, 12–19<br>1 Corinthians 11:23–26<br>John 13:1–17, 31b–35 |
| **GOOD FRIDAY** | Isaiah 52:13—53:12<br>Psalm 22<br>Hebrews 10:16–25<br>*or* 4:14–16, 5:7–9<br>John 18:1—19:42 |
| **HOLY SATURDAY** | Job 14:1–14<br>*or* Lamentations 3:1–9, 19–24<br>Psalm 31:1–4, 15–16<br>1 Peter 4:1–8<br>Matthew 27:57–66<br>*or* John 19:38–42 |

The season of Lent is forty-six days (forty, not counting Sundays). It begins on the Wednesday following Transfiguration Sunday (the last Sunday in the season of Epiphany) and lasts six weeks until the season of Easter. The primary color of the season is purple, symbolizing royalty and penitence. However, the color shifts to red on the final week, called "**Holy Week**" or "**Passion Week**." This shift occurs because it is Christ's final week leading to his death. Red is used because it is the color of blood, of passion, and of love. Black, the color of death, is used on the final two days of the season: **Good Friday** and **Holy Saturday**, or sometimes the altar is simply left bare.

## WAYS TO JOIN THE RECKONING OF LENT

### CONFESSION

If confession isn't a regular practice in your context, the season of Lent is an opportune time to utilize this ancient practice. Some evangelical contexts might have hesitations with utilizing confession. It might feel too ritualistic, create too much of what feels like a power distance between the congregation (who's confessing) and the "priest" (who's absolving), or it may just seem like too much of a downer. But when Isaiah sees the Lord in the throne room in all his glory, Isaiah confesses. "I am a man of unclean lips!" he says and is absolved by God through a coal brought by a winged creature from the altar. God then sends him out on a mission (see Isa. 6:1–8 CEB). Isaiah did not plan to confess, but when he beheld the holiness of God, he had no choice but to respond in humility.

Confession is less about our unholiness and more about God's holiness. It is less about making sure we remember all our sins—as if forgetting one will lead us to eternal damnation—and more about remembering who God is, who he made us to be, admitting we need his help to become this, and that we *have* his help in Jesus Christ. The more you know God, the more you will humbly confess because you will be reckoned or established by his holiness. If we lose sight of God, we forget any reason to confess. This is why confession is such a timely and formative practice for the church. James Smith asks,

> What is lost when we remove this chapter [confession] from so many gatherings that purport to be Christian worship? We lose an important, *counter*-formative aspect of the gospel that pushes back on secular liturgies of self-confidence that, all week long, are implicitly teaching you to "believe in yourself"—false gospels of self-assertion that refuse grace. The practice of confession is a crucial discipline for reforming our lives.[2]

Confession reorients our soul to God. In fact, this is how the prayer begins, with an address to the One whom we compare to our own life. It is more than saying, "We're bad." It is much more hopeful! You can find prescribed prayers of confession in the Book of Common Prayer as well in resources like *The Worship Sourcebook*.[3] There are a variety of confessions, some long and specific, others short and general, with language often transposed from Scripture.[4] Most often, prayers of confession follow a similar formula:

1. Address God.
2. Admit what we have done.
3. Ask for what we want (i.e., forgiveness).
4. Say why we want this.
5. Conclude the prayer.

Confessions use corporate language (we) not personal language (I), for confession is a corporate act. This is not because our personal sin isn't important, but because our personal sin can never be separated from the corporate body. The choices we make in private affect the whole body. We should not be so naïve to think *my* sin is not actually *our* sin. Therefore, when we confess, your sins are my sins, and my sins are your sins, because we are one body. And since we say this prayer together, it should be easy to read—not consisting of explicit details and long confusing phrases. Just like any corporate reading, if you're using a projector, the prayer should only be three or four slides long. The prayer should not have a clunky cadence but rather be almost poetic (i.e., rhythmic and fluid). We confess sins from our own life and sins of our society, sins of omission (when we should have done something and didn't) and sins of commission (when we shouldn't have done something and we did). As an example, take the simplicity of this confession from the Book of Common Prayer (even formatted like a poem) and notice that though it is fairly short it includes all five points mentioned earlier:

> Most merciful God,
> we confess that we have sinned against you
> in thought, word, and deed,
> by what we have done,
> and by what we have left undone.
> We have not loved you with our whole heart;
> we have not loved our neighbor as ourselves.
> We are truly sorry and we humbly repent.
> For the sake of your Son Jesus Christ,
> have mercy on us and forgive us;
> that we may delight in your will,
> and walk in your ways,
> to the glory of your Name. Amen.[5]

After confessing, we *must* be reminded of our forgiveness—assured of pardon. Never—again I say *never*—should our people confess without being offered some sort of absolution. Without an assurance of pardon we have withheld the gospel! And though the absolution only ever comes from God, we have confessed out loud, therefore we must hear the absolution out loud as well: “In Jesus’ name, we are forgiven!” If you prefer, you could sing a song of absolution. I most often prefer to use absolutions from Scripture. After a corporate prayer of confession, consider reading:

> God is so rich in mercy, and he loved us so much, that even though we were dead because of our sins, he gave us life. —Ephesians 2:4–7
>
> He has removed our sins . . . as far from us as the east is from the west. —Psalm 103:8–12
>
> Once again you will have compassion on us. You will trample our sins under your feet and throw them into the depths of the ocean! —Micah 7:18–20

I need these reminders often. I would guess our congregations need them as well. “What if we *want* to confess our sins,” asks Smith, “and didn’t even realize it until given the opportunity? In other words, what if confession is, unwittingly, the desire of every broken heart?”[6] Where else do our people get the opportunity to admit they’ve messed up and at the same time hear such hope proclaimed over them? It’s exhausting to carry guilt and shame throughout our life and so we almost always find our own ways to absolve ourselves whether we realize it or not. But our substitutes are often unhealthy, addictive, and not actually absolving at all; they're anesthetic. Corporate confession is a beautiful opportunity to admit our shortcomings and be reminded of Christ's forgiveness and love for us—especially in a season meant to reckon or establish us with our fading humanity. We turn to God, our Creator, in our weakness because he has given us something beyond ourselves to save us. He has given us himself.

## LAMENT

Lent gets darker and darker as the season progresses. At first the tension is light, but soon the religious leaders are planning ways to kill Jesus, and not long after, he is arrested in the garden and nailed to a cross. There is evil. There is confusion. There is sadness. There is death. This causes us to stop and ask, "*What* is happening? *Why* is this happening? Was there no other way? Everything seemed to be going so well; why now?" Though these questions are instigated by our journey with Christ up to this point, they sound terribly similar to the questions that accompany any of life's tragedies.

Lent provides a unique opportunity for the church: the opportunity to lament. When planning services without any annual method like the Christian Year, it isn't common for a worship director to plan a service of lament. Why would they unless there were some large-scale catastrophe? But my guess is that even while you sit and read this, numerous things come to mind that you could lament from your own life, the life of your neighbor, congregation, city, nation, and world. It gets kind of messy when we start talking about lamenting in corporate worship. A lot of questions come up that we don't have easy answers for. Therefore, it seems that the church has commonly sought to look beyond these things to the happier parts of life, perhaps suggesting to the parishioner (verbally or nonverbally) that the corporate gathering is not a place to be sad. The Christian Year, however, takes us where we often don't want to go, but we go because Christ himself went there first.

The questions provoked by lament can be scary, especially when we bear the weight of believing that if we can't provide the answers people are looking for, we have failed. But in this season, we are invited to join Peter's cries, "Lord, where are you going? . . . Why can't I come now, Lord?" Jesus doesn't offer answers, just more truths about our human capacity. "You can't go with me now. . . . I tell you the truth, Peter—before the rooster crows tomorrow morning, you will deny three time that you even know me" (John 13:31–38). In Lent, we—like Peter—have many questions and hopes that go unanswered and are left to reckon with our human reality.

The church should never be so proud as to think we fully know the answers to the realities we face. We have motifs, allegories, and ideas, like little puzzle pieces we try to fit together; but instead of answers, the season of Lent gives affirmation. We are given affirmations of our confusion instead of quippy mantras. Our questions are finally voiced by disciples and friends of Jesus. Our pain is no longer isolating, and Christ is more real to us than ever before because, in finally being permitted to embrace our pain, we discover that he knows our pain more than anyone else. The palpability of our faith hits us when we are finally allowed to bring our unhappiness to church.

Don't run away from these sad biblical experiences. To avoid them in the corporate gathering is to have an incomplete understanding of humanity and of God. Instead, lean in, watch Christ's every move, and learn how to die even as we live. Before his physical death, we see his friends abandon him. We watch as he is mocked and remains silent. We hear a mob beg for a criminal's life over his own flawless one. In all of this, he was dying and yet somehow, contradictorily, mysteriously, he was ushering in life. He was revealing what it is to be human. "If you give up your life for my sake, you will save it" (Luke 9:24). This season, then, is a season of contradictions.

If the platform (chancel) in your church is usually filled, clear it off and make it bare. Take away anything that brightens the space up—make it plain, almost treating the season like a funeral. Use dormant grass instead of flowers. If the lights are normally bright, dim them just a little (but not so much you can't see each other; it's still *corporate* worship). Use fewer instruments—try going acoustic. Maybe even use just a piano and a large group of vocalists. Include testimonies from your people that reveal God's ever-presence and giving of life within hardship. In a sense, you are creating a score and a backdrop to the story of Christ's passion: the contrast of a seemingly triumphant darkness alongside the revelation of the greatest act of love known in all the universe. God has become human—even human unto death—so that he can bring life, even life into death.

### BURY THE HALLELUJAH

One historic tradition of the church in the season of Lent is to "bury the hallelujah." The word *hallelujah* means simply, "Praise the Lord," but it is often associated with the celebration of Easter as a higher form of praise. Therefore, around the medieval era, the church began to bury the hallelujah throughout the season of Lent, omitting the word from the Lenten liturgy. Force yourself for these six weeks to omit songs, readings, and prayers that include the word *hallelujah* and you might notice a natural decrescendo in the mood of your services. A lot of songs with the word *hallelujah* are bigger and louder. If you simplify your music through this season, you and your people will feel it, and you'll find yourselves looking forward to, even yearning for, Easter morning when Lent is over and the hallelujah rises with Christ from the dead.

### HOLY WEEK

Holy Week is the final week of Lent and Christ's final week before his death. From his triumphal entry into Jerusalem, his cleansing of the temple, and his final parables, to the Sanhedrin's plot to kill him, the Lord's Supper, his eventual death, and his placement in the tomb, it is a full week and one that deserves special attention. The week begins on **Palm Sunday** and I'm sure you've experienced kids waving palm branches in the aisle while the rest of the congregation sings, "Hosanna! Loud Hosanna." What a beautiful way to facilitate intergenerational worship *and* tell the story of Christ.

However, this service should also cause us to lean into what is coming. We are still in Lent, so Palm Sunday almost acts as a teaser. People are lively, there is excitement, and Jesus is supportive of it. But not long after, we experience a dissonance to the celebration. Jesus weeps over the city, "How I wish today that you of all people would understand the way to peace. But now it is too late, and peace is hidden from your eyes. . . . You did not recognize it when God visited you" (Luke 19:41–44). If this isn't foreshadowing of some looming darkness, I don't know what is. Reality hits us and we realize that though we just celebrated Christ as our king, he is more than a just a king. He is a prophet, and he is our priest. So, though it is entirely appropriate and good to join our voices with the crowd as Jesus enters Jerusalem on Palm Sunday, we should be sure to return to the larger narrative, preparing together for the cry of the crowd about to come. For, "They kept shouting, 'Crucify him! Crucify him!'" (Luke 23:21).

So much is about to happen in the days following Palm Sunday. How often does one know that they are living the last week before their death? Holy Week captures some of Christ's final public appearances and seems like an important opportunity to encourage your congregation to engage with these specific texts. Perhaps you could create a devotional for your congregation to read the assigned texts each day, inviting different staff or parishioners to write a devotional thought to accompany each one. In my context, there are some with a great appreciation for simple vesper-like services. So, Monday through Thursday of Holy Week, we offer evening services in a small chapel area of our church, a Good Friday service on Friday, and the body does not gather while Christ is in the tomb on Holy Saturday. We sing short Taizé choruses at these small vesper services, read the lectionary passages, take Communion each night, and are then sent out. Like a suspenseful movie scene that slows down and shows every minute detail, so does Holy Week allow us to watch closely as Christ willingly walks into death.

## SPECIAL SERVICES

### ASH WEDNESDAY

Lent normally offers the greatest number of special services of any other season in the Christian Year. The first special service is offered on the first day of Lent: Ash Wednesday (always on a Wednesday, obviously, and forty-six days before the first Sunday of Easter). As mentioned earlier in this chapter, this is a time to reckon with our humanity. We confront our sin by confessing, and receive ashes as a sign of our humanity. We are absolved and fortified at the Table of our Lord. We are then sent out, called to observe a holy Lent.

### MAUNDY THURSDAY

Thursday of Holy Week is often called Maundy Thursday, referring to Jesus' new commandment (or *mandatum* in Latin) given to his disciples at the Last Supper. He told them, "Love each other. Just as I have loved you, you should love each other" (John 13:34). Some traditions, often related to the Anabaptists, offer what is known as Love Feast on this day. As the name alludes to, the service normally centers around a meal in which the eucharistic elements are included. Some traditions might even include foot washing in this service. In many high church traditions, the Maundy Thursday liturgy will end by stripping the altar so it is bare for Good Friday.

## GOOD FRIDAY

This special service is held on the Friday of Holy Week. The service is devoted to remembering the death of Christ. Where Advent and Ash Wednesday might be considered more thematic services, Good Friday centers around the specific narrative of Christ's death. In my context, this service is always held at noon, since this is the time the gospel writers tell us Jesus was crucified. There are a number of ways to facilitate this service; however, a common approach is that of stations, or movements, in which we journey with Christ through scenes leading up to his death. Though the number of stations varies across traditions, seven or fourteen tend to be the most common breakdown.

More important than any specific number of stations is the journey we take with Christ. Therefore, it might be beneficial when planning a Good Friday service to have a chart close by like the one below. This chart provides a breakdown of movements to the cross with the associated scriptural references. It is important to realize that not every Gospel includes each scene. There is some debate on the implications of this for a Good Friday service. Do you just pick and choose Gospel accounts? Do you stick with just one? I would suggest considering the role the text is playing. If it's truly a narration of the events, then it's helpful to include multiple Gospels—but if you do this, then perhaps you should always have the same voice read Matthew, a different voice read Mark, another read Luke, and yet another, John. Perhaps you could even script a scene to include multiple Gospel writers and their perspectives, almost as though they were retelling the events together.

| | MATTHEW | MARK | LUKE | JOHN |
|---|---|---|---|---|
| The Plot to Kill Jesus | 26:1–5 | 14:1–2 | | |
| Jesus Anointed at Bethany | 26:6–13 | 14:3–9 | | 12:1–11 |
| Judas Agrees to Betray Jesus | 26:14–16 | 14:10–11 | 22:1–6 | |
| The Last Supper | 26:17–35 | 14:12–31 | 22:7–38 | 13–17 |
| Preparations | 26:17–19 | 14:12–16 | 22:7–13 | |
| Jesus Washes Disciples' Feet | | | | 13:1–17 |
| Jesus Predicts His Betrayal | 26:20–25 | 14:17–21 | 22:21–23 | 13:18–30 |
| Eucharist | 26:26–30 | 14:22–26 | 22:14–20 | |
| The Disciples Argue | | | 22:24–30 | |
| Jesus Predicts Peter's Denial | 26:31–35 | 14:27–31 | 22:31–34 | 13:31–38 |
| Jesus Teaches at the Table | | | 22:35–38 | 14–16 |
| Jesus Prays at the Table | | | | 17 |
| Jesus Prays in Gethsemane | 26:36–46 | 14:32–42 | 22:39–46 | |
| Jesus is Betrayed and Arrested | 26:47–56 | 14:43–52 | 22:47–53 | 18:1–11 |
| Jesus before the Council | 26:57–68 | 14:53–65 | 22:63–71 | 18:12–14, 19–24 |
| Peter Denies Jesus | 26:69–75 | 14:66–72 | 22:54–62 | 18:15–18, 25–27 |
| Judas Hangs Himself | 27:3–10 | | | |
| Jesus' Trial before Pilate | 27:1–2, 11–26 | 15:1–15 | 23:1–25 | 18:28—19:16 |
| The Soldiers Mock Jesus | 27:27–31 | 15:16–20 | | |
| The Crucifixion | 27:32–44 | 15:21–32 | 23:26–43 | 19:17–27 |
| The Death of Jesus | 27:45–56 | 15:33–41 | 23:44–49 | 19:28–37 |

If there is a thematic point to be made, then staying within the Gospel that makes this point would be wise. Many, including the lectionary, promote the use of John in retelling Christ's passion. John contrasts light and darkness throughout his Gospel, so perhaps in a Tenebrae service—which emphasizes the gradual diminishing of light by extinguishing candles throughout the service—the Gospel of John could be used exclusively.

Once you decide what portions of the narrative you'll present, then there are many different ways to go about this retelling. Tenebrae, as mentioned before, would offer a reading and then the extinguishing of a candle and perhaps singing a hymn, similar to the flow of a Lessons and Carols service as explained in the season of Advent. You could fill the altar with symbols found within the readings and clear the altar one by one (a basin and towel, grapes, bread, wheat, a chalice, palms, the black altar cloth, and the Christ candle). You could identify the pain of Christ or specific losses and have planned testimonies from your congregation for each scene. You could pair readings of Christ's journey to the cross with other Scripture texts to emphasize the contradiction of life and death, darkness and light. The narrative is the foundation; it is your job then to creatively facilitate the retelling or reenactment of the narrative so your people can journey with Christ, mourn his suffering, and more fully know his goodness and love.

Lastly, in regard to a Good Friday service, I want to emphasize the importance of not resolving the tension of Christ's death. It is hard to leave Christ in the tomb. We know what's going to happen; it doesn't feel right not to mention it. But to skip through Christ's death to his resurrection steals one of the most human attributes from Christ. He was human. He died. His friends mourned. They didn't know in that moment the hope we know today. Therefore, we offer no corporate acknowledgment of what's to come so that we can fully experience the disciples' reality and be forced to live through the God-forsakenness of Holy Saturday. Every year our service ends with "and he breathed his last." The Christ candle is extinguished, and the congregation is left in complete darkness (except for what light comes through the stained-glass windows). No announcement or sending is offered. The bulletin simply states, "At the conclusion of this service, you are invited to stay as long as you desire. When you leave, please leave in silence. We will gather once again on Sunday to remember the rest of the story."

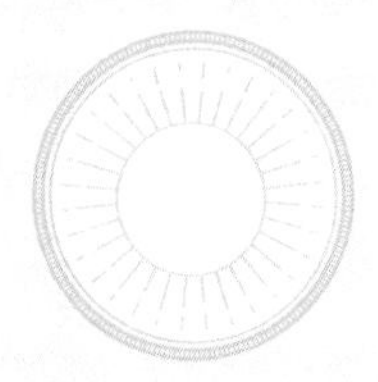

# EASTER

## The Invitation to Triumph with Christ over Sin and Death

### TIME

50 days
*following the season of Lent*

### COLOR

White with gold accent
*(color of joy and celebration)*

### SPECIAL DAYS

- **Easter Sunday** (the first Sunday of the season of Easter)
- **Ascension Day** (the fortieth day of Easter; often celebrated the following Sunday)
- **Pentecost** (the fiftieth day—the eighth and final Sunday—of Easter)
  *Color changes to red (color of fire, symbolizing the Holy Spirit)*

"Early on Sunday morning, while it was still dark, Mary Magdalene came to the tomb and found that the stone had been rolled away from the entrance" (John 20:1–18). We thought the climax of this story was our Lord's death. It was supposed to be finished. Weren't those even his final words on the cross? Normally, after a main character dies, all that remains in the narrative is the resolution for those left behind. But in Christ's life, he finished one story so he could start another—a story in which death was no longer the end.

Early on that Sunday morning, Mary witnessed the ushering in of a new era that would last for eternity: the era of triumph. God, who saw the captivity of his people—being held hostage by the devil—gave himself up, as Athanasius writes, "to settle man's account with death and free him from the primal transgression."[1] Christ had come "to bear the curse that lay on us; and how could He 'become a curse' otherwise than by accepting the accursed death?"[2] Almost as a divine comedy, God revealed that though he had abided by the devil's rules of the game (that is, death)—and therefore remained true to his righteous nature, even to the unrighteous—death was still no match for God.[3]

"Death is swallowed up in victory. O death, where is your victory? O death, where is your sting?" (1 Cor. 15:54b–55, ref. Isa. 25:8 and Hos. 13:14). Isaiah, Hosea, and Paul taunt death. The epidemic of dying is mocked—it is not as powerful as we once thought it was. Athanasius wrote, "Before the divine sojourn of the Savior, even the holiest of men were afraid of death, and mourned the dead as those who perish. But now that the Savior has raised His body, death is no longer terrible, but all those who believe in Christ tread it underfoot as nothing."[4] Death no longer has the final word. Somehow, by some mystery, by some divine power, death became just one step in the journey of even more life. "So you see, just as death came into the world through a man, now the resurrection from the dead has begun through another man. Just as everyone dies because we all belong to Adam, everyone who belongs to Christ will be given new life" (1 Cor. 15:21–22).

In the grand picture of life, every day after this day is Easter. Easter is the Christian reality—the foundation of the church. From this point in history, we realize that the kingdom of heaven is "eastering" all around us whether we identify it or not.[5] Like cracks in the pavement as vegetation sticks its head out—life in the earth can't help but break through human infrastructure to reclaim its own. Even in our own lives, Easter is breaking in. We can either make room for it or watch our lives crumble apart as it breaks through our attempts to direct it.

This is exciting news! The climax is not just that we are saved *from* something (i.e., our sin), but Christ reveals through the resurrection that we are also saved *for* something (i.e., abundant life).[6] If all we're looking for is a covering of our sin, abundant life will be shocking, painful, maybe even blasphemous, as it breaks through our human-made structures and overruns our realities. We'll spend our lives working against it, saying, "No, you can't invade, ruin, or change this part of my life!" But for those that look beyond forgiveness, they will see a salvation that cannot be bound to one moment but instead lasts more than a lifetime. It will take them places they did not think to go and would not have chosen on their own. This salvation *is* life and nothing can keep life down, not even death. They join those before them and those after them on the journey to the promised land, each step realizing more fully the promise of sharing in Christ's divine nature, escaping the world's corruption (see 2 Peter 1:4). In the season of Easter, we begin again. This time, not with Adam as our source of identity, but the living Christ.

| | YEAR A | YEAR B | YEAR C |
|---|---|---|---|
| **WEEK 1** | Acts 10:34–43<br>*or* Jeremiah 31:1–6<br>Psalm 118:1–2, 14–24<br>Colossians 3:1–4<br>*or* Acts 10:34–43<br>John 20:1–18<br>*or* Matthew 28:1–10 | Acts 10:34–43<br>*or* Isaiah 25:6-9<br>Psalm 118:1–2, 14–24<br>1 Corinthians 15:1–11<br>*or* Acts 10:34–43<br>John 20:1–18<br>*or* Mark 16:1–8 | Acts 10:34–43<br>*or* Isaiah 65:17–25<br>Psalm 118:1–2, 14–24<br>1 Corinthians 15:19–26<br>*or* Acts 10:34–43<br>John 20:1–18<br>*or* Luke 24:1–12 |
| **WEEK 2** | Acts 2:14a, 22–32<br>Psalm 16<br>1 Peter 1:3–9<br>John 20:19–31 | Acts 4:32–35<br>Psalm 133<br>1 John 1:1—2:2<br>John 20:19–31 | Acts 5:27–32<br>Psalm 118:14–29 *or* 150<br>Revelation 1:4–8<br>John 20:19–31 |
| **WEEK 3** | Acts 2:14a, 36–41<br>Psalm 116:1–4, 12–19<br>1 Peter 1:17–23<br>Luke 24:13–35 | Acts 3:12–19<br>Psalm 4<br>1 John 3:1–7<br>Luke 24:36b–48 | Acts 9:1–6 (7–20)<br>Psalm 30<br>Revelation 5:11–14<br>John 21:1–19 |
| **WEEK 4** | Acts 2:42–47<br>Psalm 23<br>1 Peter 2:19–25<br>John 10:1–10 | Acts 4:5–12<br>Psalm 23<br>1 John 3:16–24<br>John 10:11–18 | Acts 9:36–43<br>Psalm 23<br>Revelation 7:9–17<br>John 10:22–30 |
| **WEEK 5** | Acts 7:55–60<br>Psalm 31:1–5, 15–16<br>1 Peter 2:2–10<br>John 14:1–14 | Acts 8:26–40<br>Psalm 22:25–31<br>1 John 4:7–21<br>John 15:1–8 | Acts 11:1–18<br>Psalm 148<br>Revelation 21:1–6<br>John 13:31–35 |
| **WEEK 6** | Acts 17:22–31<br>Psalm 66:8–20<br>1 Peter 3:13–22<br>John 14:15–21 | Acts 10:44–48<br>Psalm 98<br>1 John 5:1–6<br>John 15:9–17 | Acts 16:9–15<br>Psalm 67<br>Revelation 21:10, 22:1–5<br>John 14:23–29<br>*or* John 5:1–9 |
| **THE ASCENSION**<br>*40th Day of Easter* | Acts 1:1–11<br>Psalm 47 *or* 93<br>Ephesians 1:15–23<br>Luke 24:44–53 | | |

| | YEAR A | YEAR B | YEAR C |
|---|---|---|---|
| **WEEK 7** *Ascension Sunday* | Acts 1:6–14<br>Psalm 68:1–10, 32–35<br>1 Peter 4:12–14, 5:6–11<br>John 17:1–11 | Acts 1:15–17, 21–26<br>Psalm 1<br>1 John 5:9–13<br>John 17:6–19 | Acts 16:16–34<br>Psalm 97<br>Revelation 22:12–14, 16–17, 20–21<br>John 17:20–26 |
| **PENTECOST SUNDAY** | | | |
| **WEEK 8** | Acts 2:1–21<br>*or* Numbers 11:24–30<br>Psalm 104:24–34, 35b<br>1 Corinthians 12:3b–13<br>*or* Acts 2:1–21<br>John 20:19–23<br>*or* 7:37–39 | Acts 2:1–21<br>*or* Ezekiel 37:1–14<br>Psalm 104:24–34, 35b<br>Romans 8:22–27<br>*or* Acts 2:1–21<br>John 15:26–27; 16:4b–15 | Acts 2:1–21<br>*or* Genesis 11:1–9<br>Psalm 104:24–34, 35b<br>Romans 8:14–17<br>*or* Acts 2:1–21<br>John 14:8–17 (25–27) |

The first half of the Christian Year tells the story of Christ's coming and life on earth (Advent, Christmas, Epiphany, Lent, and Easter). The last half tells the story of Christ's life in and through the church (Ordinary Time). Easter is the longest season in the first half of the Christian Year (Christ's life on earth). It is not just one day, but fifty! So, I hope you hid a lot of eggs because that's one long Easter egg hunt. The color of the season is white since, similar to Christmas, it is a time of great celebration.

## WAYS TO JOIN THE TRIUMPH OF EASTER

### START WHERE YOU LEFT OFF

Many times, **Easter Sunday**—the first Sunday of the Easter season—will start loud, full, and bright. This makes sense and is even appropriate for the season, especially if you've pulled back and darkened your services throughout Lent. However, if you offered a Good Friday service, or if you know that many of your people attended a Good Friday service somewhere else, you might want to consider starting your Easter Sunday service where things ended. It's not wrong to walk into a sanctuary on Easter Sunday and just know, "Yep, Christ is alive." But how often do we corporately experience that scene played out together? We know the full story now, but when Mary went to the tomb early that morning while it was still dark, she was expecting Christ to still be dead. The possibility hadn't crossed her mind that he could in fact be alive.

What if your people walked into a dark sanctuary (similar to how they may have left it on Good Friday)? Perhaps you could even begin with a song that recalls the events of Good Friday. But then, someone comes forward and says,

> When the Sabbath was over, Mary Magdalene, Mary the mother of James, and Salome bought spices so that they could go and anoint Jesus' dead body. Early in the morning of the first day of the week, while it was still dark, Mary Magdalene came to the tomb.
>
> —Mark 16:1; John 20:1 (CEB)

At this point, while the reading continues, the lights could begin to fade up and the music and rhythm grow to express the intensity of the earthquake that rolled the stone away.

> On the way they were asking each other, "Who will roll away the stone for us from the entrance to the tomb?" Suddenly there was a great earthquake! For an angel of the Lord came down from heaven, rolled aside the stone, and sat on it.
>
> —Mark 16:3; Matthew 28:2

Then with lights at full brightness and instruments at full volume, the reader could boldly proclaim:

> The angel said to the women, "Do not be afraid, for I know that you are looking for Jesus, who was crucified. He is not here; he has risen!"
> —Matthew 28:5–6; Luke 24:6 (NIV)

At this point, you could go into a familiar song proclaiming the resurrection of Christ.

There are numerous songs that tell the full story of the cross to the grave to the resurrection, so with some musical creativity you might be able to blend these Scriptures with a full song. You could then read some parts of the story and sing other parts. Triumph is more fully realized when it is presented in the face of defeat. Though everyone walking in on Easter Sunday may intellectually be aware that Christ was dead and that now he is alive, how often do we get to experience the stark contrast of realities—how often do we get to relive re-creation? One moment life seemed meaningless, trivial, and hopeless, but within a matter of minutes Mary's whole world was flipped upside down as once again, in a garden, there was a new beginning.

## RESURRECT THE HALLELUJAH

As mentioned in the Lenten chapter, it is common to bury the hallelujah during that season, but in the season of Easter this proclamation of praise should resurrect with Christ and be proclaimed throughout. Sing it, say it, preach it, pray it! Many of the songs that include the word *Hallelujah* fit the celebratory and triumphant nature of the season of Easter, Charles Wesley's "Christ the Lord Is Risen Today" being a prime example.

## "CHRIST IS RISEN! HE IS RISEN INDEED!"

I'm sure you've heard the popular greeting, "Christ is risen!" and the people respond, "He is risen indeed!" This is commonly used on Easter Sunday, but I encourage you to keep using it all eight Sundays! Your people will probably ask, "Why are we still saying that? Wasn't Easter weeks ago?" What a great opportunity to not only enter into a discussion on Easter as a season, but also on the prominence of what is happening in this season. As mentioned earlier, the Christian church is founded on the events of Easter. Without Easter, there would be no Christian church. Our faith is established on the fact that Christ is *still* alive. As Paul wrote, "If Christ has not been raised, then all our preaching is useless, and your faith is useless" (1 Cor. 15:14). Looking outside the Christian Year for a moment, every Sunday is an Easter Sunday. Living on this side of the resurrection, every time the church gathers it is because of the resurrection. So, then, when using the Christian Year to tell the narrative of Christ throughout one year, is it not appropriate to take at least fifty days of 365 to elevate this portion of the story of God? Let's celebrate this cornerstone of our faith for an entire season. Christ is risen! (Go ahead, say it out loud): "He is risen indeed!"

Every local church has its own contextual values. One context I knew was very conscious of their sanitary practices during worship services. Therefore, during flu season it was important to make certain adjustments to their service structure to accommodate this value. This resulted in the removal of the weekly greeting time during flu season. However, they sought to lean into this concern and used the greeting-hiatus to play to the advantage of telling the story of Christ. Though technically flu season in this particular part of the world stretched from around November to the end of March, the highest points of the season were typically in February and March—commonly the months within the season of Lent. Therefore, in playing into the ethos of the season, they removed the greeting time from their liturgy during Lent. But, just as flu season ended, they welcomed in the season of Easter and did so by resurrecting the corporate greeting time. Though they never called explicit attention to their intentionality, there was a subconscious lifting of the mood in welcoming Easter. Not only is death contrasted with life at the turn of Easter, but personal reckoning and contemplation is contrasted with ecumenical celebration and triumph through turning to those seated around you and greeting them with the peace of the resurrected Lord.

## BEING MADE NEW

The season of Easter centers on new life triumphing over the old. Primarily we celebrate this in Christ's life, but this season is also a time to recognize the implications of Christ's life on our own lives. Easter is a great season to include testimonies that reveal God's nature to make all things new. The church should never lose sight of God's continued work to transform us even after our primary conversion. Don't only make room in your services to share these stories, help your people put them into words.

I realize there is often a lot of hesitancy, even fear, surrounding testimonies. Who knows what the people will say? What if they take the mic and go on some political rant or they simply never stop talking? It happens; I get it. But I think a lot of this can be avoided if we treat testimonies as an art. Not many people can pick up a paintbrush and create a beautiful mural their first try. Yet, we expect our parishioners to be able to string words together in front of a congregation without honing the craft. Art takes practice. So, if in the past you've just opened up the floor, perhaps you could be a bit more intentional with helping your parishioners prepare testimonies.

Sit down with your people, listen to their stories, and help them understand what God has been doing in them by asking questions: Who were you before? Who are you now? What moments, conversations, or experiences did God use to get you from there to here? I'm not talking exclusively conversion stories. I'm talking about any journey in which God changes the disposition of a person. From the addict's new healthy habits to the big brother that used to get mad at his siblings but has learned to appreciate and even, at times, enjoy them—God's life never stops transforming our subhuman ways into becoming fountains of life to the world around us.

Select eight people—one per week of the season—to share how they've experienced the life of Christ affecting their own life and help them learn how to share these testimonies. It takes work to compose a testimony—to tell a story while ensuring that the story never loses focus on the primacy of God's activity. What details should be included? What was important to the individual but isn't necessary for the corporate body? What attributes of God were revealed more fully to them in this process? What Christlike attribute did God develop in them through this work? It isn't an easy process. Remember, it's an art.

Perhaps in a more casual setting you could invite people to offer live testimonies from pre-planned prompts. Post a list of ten attributes of God and ask people to share testimonies using one of the attributes listed. Perhaps you could even give them the prompt, "God has revealed his (insert attribute: love, patience, justice, peace, joy, etc.) to me through . . . ." Many resources exist that can offer methods for crafting testimonies.[7] It is a fruitful craft in our journey of faith; I can think of many occasions that I have been greatly encouraged by someone else's journey with God.

Learning to talk about God's activity translates beyond the corporate gathering as well. If you've put in the time to wrestle through writing a testimony, it will be that much easier for you to contextualize it, whether you're in front of an entire congregation, a classroom, or just with a friend at a coffee shop. Christ is alive and active among us. If we don't have testimonies to share the ways we've seen his presence at work, either we haven't been looking for it, we don't know him well enough to identify the work as his, or no one's ever helped us—or given us the invitation—to articulate it.

## VISIBLE SIGNS OF INVISIBLE GRACE

Finally, celebrate the sacraments! Augustine called the sacraments "visible signs" of "invisible grace."[8] God gives himself to us in a peculiar way through the purifying waters of baptism and through the bread and cup at his table.[9] In alignment with the new life of Easter, baptism is a beautiful act of new birth. We are dead to sin, and alive in Christ Jesus! Before they go under the waters, invite those about to be baptized to share a testimony of God's work in their life. If it is an infant baptism, invite the parents to share a testimony of how they have experienced Christ through the body of believers before they celebrate their child's rebirth into the Christian community. As suggested in the earlier chapter on the season of Epiphany, it is also appropriate to invite your congregation to remember their baptism throughout the season of Easter by setting out fonts of the baptismal waters.

Celebrate the Eucharist. Come to the table knowing it is there that Christ offers us his life—it is a divine meal of triumph! It should go without saying that the Eucharist (coming from the Greek word meaning "thanksgiving") should never be celebrated without mentioning the resurrection. No matter what season it is, we come to a table that is past, present, and future to partake not of death, but of the life of our risen Lord. So, tell the full story at the table. Death has been defeated by Christ, and now, in the bread and the cup, he offers us himself so that we may then take him to a hungry world.

Whatever you do, boldly embrace the triumph of these fifty days, remembering, proclaiming, and thanking God, looking forward to the ever-Eastering work of the Father in Christ through the power of the Holy Spirit.

## SPECIAL SERVICES

### THE EASTER VIGIL

Similar to the welcoming in of Christmas, some traditions will offer an Easter Vigil to welcome this season following Lent. The vigil begins as "a wake (recalling Christ in the tomb)," explains Constance Cherry, "and ends with the announcement of the resurrection (recalling Christ's triumph)." Traditionally, Christian converts would go through a process of instruction called catechesis during the season of Lent. Therefore, the Easter Vigil would act as the culmination of this process and "became the occasion for the baptism of catechumenates early in the life of the church."[10] Beyond this one special service, the season of Easter emphasizes the Sunday service itself; after all, it is because of the resurrection that Christians gather on Sundays. Therefore, the following "special services" might be more appropriately titled "special Sundays."

### THE FIRST TWO WEEKS

As is true in many of the seasons, each Sunday is prescribed a certain theme through the lectionary's selected texts. For example, the first Sunday of Easter is *the* Easter Sunday on which we retell the immediate events surrounding the stone being rolled away. The second Sunday is often referred to as "**Doubting Thomas Sunday**." Just as the beginning of the Christmas season is promptly contrasted by the darkness of the massacre of the Holy Innocents, Thomas similarly reminds us that the whole world wasn't in agreement about what had just happened. Thomas wanted proof and Christ gave him himself. Thomas stands in for many of us today and though we may not have been given the invitation to put our hands in Christ's wounds, what Christ did for Thomas he did, in that moment, for all who doubt.

## THE ASCENSION

The fortieth day of Easter is known as Ascension Day and is often commemorated on the Sunday following (i.e., the seventh Sunday of the season). On this day, we remember Christ's ascension into heaven. As we watch him ascend, we hear the voices of two men dressed in white that suddenly appear: "Why are you standing here staring into heaven? Jesus has been taken from you into heaven, but someday he will return from heaven in the same way you saw him go!" (Acts 1:10–11).

What a bizarre experience, and yet this story is filled with foundational ecclesiology and eschatology. It's a story we need to remember. Perhaps you could retell the story by having three people representing Matthew, Mark, and Luke share it in first person, as though it had just happened (perhaps you could even ask the readers to memorize their lines).

***Luke:*** *When we were with Jesus, we kept asking him, "Lord, has the time come for you to free Israel and restore our kingdom?"*

*He told us, "The Father alone has the authority to set those dates and times, and they are not for you to know. But you will receive power when the Holy Spirit comes upon you. And you will be my witnesses" (Acts 1:6–8a).*

***Mark:*** He said, "Go into all the world and preach the Good News to everyone. Anyone who believes and is baptized will be saved. But anyone who refuses to believe will be condemned" (Mark 16:15–16).

***Matthew:*** *He told us, "Teach these new disciples to obey all the commands I have given you. And be sure of this: I am with you always, even to the end of the age" (Matt. 28:20).*

***Luke:*** After saying this, he was taken up into a cloud while we were watching, and we could no longer see him. As we strained to see him rising into heaven, two white-robed men suddenly stood among us. "People of Galilee," they said, "why are you standing here staring into heaven? Jesus has been taken from you into heaven, but someday he will return from heaven in the same way you saw him go!" (Acts 1:9–11).

## PENTECOST

Gathered around a table with his friends on the night he would be betrayed, Jesus told his disciples, "I will ask the Father, and he will give you another Advocate, who will never leave you. He is the Holy Spirit, who leads into all truth. The world cannot receive him, because it isn't looking for him and doesn't recognize him. But you know him, because he lives *with* you now and later will be *in* you" (John 14:16–17, emphasis added). There is a significant difference between God with us and God in us, yet Luke writes that "On the day of Pentecost all the believers were meeting together in one place. Suddenly, there was a sound from heaven . . . and everyone present was filled with the Holy Spirit" (Acts 2:1–4). It was already countercultural for God to dwell with his people in a tabernacle. Then he broke all god-stereotypes by becoming like his creation in the human Jesus Christ. But now, on Pentecost Sunday, we celebrate God taking up residence *in* his people.

Consider your unique identity—your skills, knowledge, position, resources, relationships, and personality. How might these things be enacted if God fully dwelt in you? How would your concerns change? How would you speak? How would you treat others? How would you use your time and money? How would you interpret the things that happen around you? Pentecost reveals God's desire to fully dwell within us and it calls us (in Ordinary Time) to do the hard work of making room for him.

Pentecost is a bridge between the final Sunday of Easter and the beginning of Ordinary Time. Just as the "eighth day" of the week is both the end of the previous week and the beginning of the new week, Pentecost is the eighth Sunday of Easter and not only concludes the season (and the first half of the Christian Year) but marks the beginning of the remainder of the year and the life of Christ in the church.[11] The word *pentecost* comes from the Greek word *pentékoste*, which means fiftieth. This is fitting as Pentecost is the fiftieth and final day of Easter. Though numerous people were self-proclaimed Christ-followers prior to this day, it is on Pentecost that the church as a global movement is considered to have been born.

Besides being a day to celebrate the Holy Spirit dwelling in us, Pentecost offers a rather heightened experiential moment with God. Sounds from heaven like the roaring of a mighty windstorm, flames or tongues of fire settling on the believers, the ability to speak in other languages—I mean, come on—this is exciting stuff! So exciting, if we're honest, that we've probably wished we could have experienced it ourselves. Perhaps you have experienced something like it. Miraculous testimonies of God stepping outside the boundaries of natural order are not extinct. But some of us may have not been privy to such an experience in our lifetime. Now, there are traditions that thrive off of seeking these experiences out, while other people share of experiences where they ran into God when they weren't even looking for him. John Wesley himself, the man my denomination is named after, speaks of having his very own heart-warming experience. A pursuit for the same experience has fueled evangelicals ever since.

Robert Webber, in his book *The Divine Embrace*, responds to this desire for a Pentecost-moment. He likens the scene at Pentecost to a first-generation Christian's dramatic encounter with Christ. He writes, "It seems . . . that this kind of dramatic change of direction is associated more with first-generation Christians, those who are first in their family's recent past to renounce Satan and all his ways and to pick up their cross daily as they turned to serve Christ."[12] Many second-, third-, and fourth-generation Christians don't have these life-altering moments and it isn't because they didn't repent well enough or pray hard enough. Those before them had already set them on the right path. They still needed to decide to walk that path and stay on that path, but hearing, "Stay on this road," will always be less dramatic than hearing, "Do a U-turn!" But for those of you who, like Webber, are still asking, "Where is that life-changing identity for us?"—Pentecost is for you.

Perhaps you know the Pentecost moment in your family's history. Maybe you were the one to have that Pentecost moment. Or, if you're like me and don't know the story of the first convert in your family, let this be your story (artistic interpretations and all):

***Reader:*** On the day of Pentecost all the believers were meeting together in one place. Suddenly, there was a sound from heaven (Acts 2:1–2).

*Instruments create a "loud sound from heaven" (a cacophony of notes and rhythms that fade into a choir or select voices making wind sounds,* "Shhhhhhhh").

It was like the roaring of a mighty windstorm, and it filled the house where they were sitting (2:2).

*Voices decrescendo and fade out completely. Wind chimes (or high piano arpeggios) begin softly in the background. The color shifts to red on this special day—symbolizing the Holy Spirit and fire—so, this might be a great time to have someone dance a red cloth to the altar.*

Then, what looked like flames or tongues of fire appeared and settled on each of them. And everyone present was filled with the Holy Spirit and began speaking in other languages, as the Holy Spirit gave them this ability (2:3–4).

*Voices/Choir begin repeating,* "Jesus is Lord" *in different languages, fading out as the reading continues.*

At that time there were devout Jews from every nation living in Jerusalem. When they heard the loud noise, everyone came running, and they were bewildered to hear their own languages being spoken by the believers.

They were completely amazed and exclaimed,

***People:*** "How can this be? These people are all from Galilee, and yet we hear them speaking in our own native languages about the wonderful things God had done!"

***Reader:*** They stood there amazed and perplexed.

Then Peter [preached] for a long time, strongly urging all his listeners, "Save yourselves from this crooked generation!" Those who believed what Peter said were baptized and added to the church that day—about 3,000 in all (see Acts 2:5–8, 11–12, 40–41).

Not to compare stories or anything, but I think this conversion experience beats them all when it comes to the dramatic. However, beyond Pentecost being one epic "heartwarming experience," Pentecost also reminds us that our faith is not something we possess as much as it is something that possesses us. It is bigger than us, older than us, and more diverse than us. Consider the similarities and contrasts between the story of the tower of Babel in Genesis 11 and the story of Pentecost. In the first, God used the diversity of language to confuse the people and cause disunity. In the second, God didn't put an end to the diversity, but rather used diversity to bring a unity centered not in language or culture but in story and in faith.[13]

Of any Sunday to embrace the diversity of the ecumenical church, Pentecost encourages the inclusion of other languages and other cultures' worship practices. For "there is one Lord, one faith, one baptism, one God and Father of all, who is over all, in all, and living through all" (Eph. 4:5–6). These elements should be presented respectfully, with care, and in such a way that teaches your context to value and appreciate parts of the global church that they may not interact with every day. Or you could give representation to cultures within your context that are often underrepresented (though I would argue that this should be a more regular practice already). The day of Pentecost is a Sunday to celebrate the whole church—past, present, future, local, and global, and it is a catalyst for the final and longest season of the Christian Year: the season of Ordinary Time.

# ORDINARY TIME

## The Invitation to Commit to Christ through the Church

### TIME

Begins after Pentecost
*continues to the start of the new Christian Year in Advent*

### COLOR

Green
*(color of growth)*

### SPECIAL DAYS

- **Trinity Sunday** (the first Sunday in Ordinary Time)
  *Color changes to white (color of joy and celebration)*
- **World Communion Sunday** (the first Sunday of October)
- **All Saints' Sunday** (the Sunday following November 1)
  *Color changes to white (color of joy and celebration)*
- **Christ the King Sunday** (the last Sunday of the Christian Year)
  *Color changes to gold (the color of sovereignty)*

Ordinary Time is anything but ordinary. Though, I must admit, the name doesn't really help it out. Some choose to refer to the season as "Time after Pentecost," which certainly leaves less ambiguity. But I think there is actually something beautiful in its somewhat lackluster name. Right before he ascended into heaven, Jesus said to his own disciples, "Go and make disciples of all the nations, baptizing them in the name of the Father and the Son and the Holy Spirit. Teach these new disciples to obey all the commands I have given you. And be sure of this: I am with you always, even to the end of the age" (Matt. 28:19–20). Then, on Pentecost, this calling was realized by the indwelling of the Holy Spirit. Christ's call was extraordinary—especially as we saw it play out in Pentecost—and yet it has been the call of every Christian for millennia. Constance Cherry explains it like this: "'Ordinary' refers to the ongoing work of the church to spread the message of Jesus Christ—his teaching, healing, restoration, reconciliation, forgiveness, etc.—the ordinary work and ministry expected of Christ's followers."[1] Ordinary Time reminds and exhorts us to live out Christ's basic, fundamental, ordinary expectations of us.

Therefore, the season is a season of commitment: commitment to Christ, to neighbor, even to self—to live intentionally for the betterment of the community. In an ever-growing individualistic world, the season of Ordinary Time offers a much-needed reminder that we are part of a body. After journeying with Christ over the last six months, we are right to ask the same question asked in the introduction of this book, "Who do I want to be?" (or perhaps more appropriately, "Who am I called to be?"). But I think God is inviting us to ask a bigger question in this season as well. That is, "Who are *we* called to be?"

The contemporary Western church loves using language about one's *personal* relationship with Christ. Ordinary Time, in addition to our personal relationship, invites us to consider our *corporate* relationship with Christ. It's easy to quote Paul's exhortation to "give your bodies to God" as a "living and holy sacrifice," and raise our hands higher during a worship song (see Rom. 12:1). But when Paul explains what this means for the believers, we gain a lens by which to assess our corporate relationship with God. "Don't think you are better than you really are (v. 3)." "Don't just pretend to love others. Really love them" (v. 9). "Never be lazy, but work hard and serve the Lord enthusiastically. Rejoice in our confident hope. When God's people are in need, be ready to help them. Always be eager to practice hospitality" (vv. 11–13). "Bless those who persecute you. . . . Be happy with those who are happy, and weep with those who weep. Live in harmony with each other. Don't be too proud to enjoy the company of ordinary people. And don't think you know it all! . . . Do all that you can to live in peace with everyone" (vv. 14–18). Though we are the church throughout the whole year, Ordinary Time explicitly reminds us to be the church in our ordinary everyday lives.

| | YEAR A | YEAR B | YEAR C |
|---|---|---|---|
| **TRINITY SUNDAY** *(replaces assigned Proper each year)* | | | |
| *First Sunday after Pentecost* | Genesis 1:1—2:4a<br>Psalm 8<br>2 Corinthians 13:11–13<br>Matthew 28:16–20 | Isaiah 6:1–8<br>Psalm 29<br>Romans 8:12–17<br>John 3:1–17 | Proverbs 8:1–4, 22–31<br>Psalm 8<br>Romans 5:1–5<br>John 16:12–15 |
| **PROPER 1**<br>*Sunday from May 8—May 14* | Deuteronomy 30:15–20<br>Psalm 119:1–8<br>1 Corinthians 3:1–9<br>Matthew 5:21–37 | 2 Kings 5:1–14<br>Psalm 30<br>1 Corinthians 9:24–27<br>Mark 1:40–45 | Jeremiah 17:5–10<br>Psalm 1<br>1 Corinthians 15:12–20<br>Luke 6:17–26 |

| | YEAR A | YEAR B | YEAR C |
|---|---|---|---|
| **PROPER 2**<br>*Sunday from May 15—May 21* | Leviticus 19:1–2, 9–18<br>Psalm 119:33–40<br>1 Corinthians 3:10–11, 16–23<br>Matthew 5:38–48 | Isaiah 43:18–25<br>Psalm 41<br>2 Corinthians 1:18–22<br>Mark 2:1–12 | Genesis 45:3–11, 15<br>Psalm 37:1–11, 39–40<br>1 Corinthians 15:35–38, 42–50<br>Luke 6:27–38 |
| **PROPER 3**<br>*Sunday from May 22—May 28* | Isaiah 49:8–16a<br>Psalm 131<br>1 Corinthians 4:1–5<br>Matthew 6:24–34 | Hosea 2:14–20<br>Psalm 103:1–13, 22<br>2 Corinthians 3:1–6<br>Mark 2:13–22 | Isaiah 55:10–13<br>Psalm 92:1–4, 12–15<br>1 Corinthians 15:51–58<br>Luke 6:39–49 |
| **PROPER 4**<br>*Sunday from May 29—June 4* | Deuteronomy 11:18–21, 26–28<br>Psalm 31:1–5, 19–24<br>Romans 1:16–17; 3:22b–28 (29–31)<br>Matthew 7:21–29 | Deuteronomy 5:12–15<br>Psalm 81:1–10<br>2 Corinthians 4:5–12<br>Mark 2:23—3:6 | 1 Kings 8:22–23, 41–43<br>Psalm 96:1–9<br>Galatians 1:1–12<br>Luke 7:1–10 |
| **PROPER 5**<br>*Sunday from June 5—June 11* | Hosea 5:15—6:6<br>Psalm 50:7–15<br>Romans 4:13–25<br>Matthew 9:9–13, 18–26 | Genesis 3:8–15<br>Psalm 130<br>2 Corinthians 4:13—5:1<br>Mark 3:20–35 | 1 Kings 17:17–24<br>Psalm 30<br>Galatians 1:11–24<br>Luke 7:11–17 |
| **PROPER 6**<br>*Sunday from June 12—June 18* | Exodus 19:2–8a<br>Psalm 100<br>Romans 5:1–8<br>Matthew 9:35—10:8 (9–23) | Ezekiel 17:22–24<br>Psalm 92:1–4, 12–15<br>2 Corinthians 5:6–10 (11–13), 14–17<br>Mark 4:26–34 | 2 Samuel 11:26—12:10, 13–15<br>Psalm 32<br>Galatians 2:15–21<br>Luke 7:36—8:3 |
| **PROPER 7**<br>*Sunday from June 19—June 25* | Jeremiah 20:7–13<br>Psalm 69:7–10 (11–15), 16–18<br>Romans 6:1b–11<br>Matthew 10:24–39 | Job 38:1–11<br>Psalm 107:1–3, 23–32<br>2 Corinthians 6:1–13<br>Mark 4:35–41 | Isaiah 65:1–9<br>Psalm 22:19–28<br>Galatians 3:23–29<br>Luke 8:26–39 |
| **PROPER 8**<br>*Sunday from June 26—July 2* | Jeremiah 28:5–9<br>Psalm 89:1–4, 15–18<br>Romans 6:12–23<br>Matthew 10:40–42 | Lamentations 3:22–33<br>Psalm 30<br>2 Corinthians 8:7–15<br>Mark 5:21–43 | 1 Kings 19:15–16, 19–21<br>Psalm 16<br>Galatians 5:1, 13–25<br>Luke 9:51–62 |
| **PROPER 9**<br>*Sunday from July 3—July 9* | Zechariah 9:9–12<br>Psalm 145:8–14<br>Romans 7:15–25a<br>Matthew 11:16–19, 25–30 | Ezekiel 2:1–5<br>Psalm 123<br>2 Corinthians 12:2–10<br>Mark 6:1–13 | Isaiah 66:10–14<br>Psalm 66:1–9<br>Galatians 6:(1–6) 7–16<br>Luke 10:1–11, 16–20 |

| | YEAR A | YEAR B | YEAR C |
|---|---|---|---|
| **PROPER 10**<br>*Sunday from July 10—July 16* | Isaiah 55:10–13<br>Psalm 65:(1–8) 9–13<br>Romans 8:1–11<br>Matthew 13:1–9, 18–23 | Amos 7:7–15<br>Psalm 85:8–13<br>Ephesians 1:3–14<br>Mark 6:14–29 | Deuteronomy 30:9–14<br>Psalm 25:1–10<br>Colossians 1:1–14<br>Luke 10:25–37 |
| **PROPER 11**<br>*Sunday from July 17—July 23* | Isaiah 44:6–8<br>Psalm 86:11–17<br>Romans 8:12–25<br>Matthew 13:24–30, 36–43 | Jeremiah 23:1–6<br>Psalm 23<br>Ephesians 2:11–22<br>Mark 6:30–34, 53–56 | Genesis 18:1–10a<br>Psalm 15<br>Colossians 1:15–28<br>Luke 10:38–42 |
| **PROPER 12**<br>*Sunday from July 24—July 30* | 1 Kings 3:5–12<br>Psalm 119:129–136<br>Romans 8:26–39<br>Matthew 13:31–33, 44–52 | 2 Kings 4:42–44<br>Psalm 145:10–18<br>Ephesians 3:14–21<br>John 6:1–21 | Genesis 18:20–32<br>Psalm 138<br>Colossians 2:6–15 (16–19)<br>Luke 11:1–13 |
| **PROPER 13**<br>*Sunday from July 31—Aug. 6* | Isaiah 55:1–5<br>Psalm 145:8–9, 14–21<br>Romans 9:1–5<br>Matthew 14:13–21 | Exodus 16:2–4, 9–15<br>Psalm 78:23–29<br>Ephesians 4:1–16<br>John 6:24–35 | Ecclesiastes 1:2, 12–14; 2:18–23<br>Psalm 49:1–12<br>Colossians 3:1–11<br>Luke 12:13–21 |
| **PROPER 14**<br>*Sunday from Aug. 7—Aug. 13* | 1 Kings 19:9–18<br>Psalm 85:8–13<br>Romans 10:5–15<br>Matthew 14:22–33 | 1 Kings 19:4–8<br>Psalm 34:1–8<br>Ephesians 4:25—5:2<br>John 6:35, 41–51 | Genesis 15:1–6<br>Psalm 33:12–22<br>Hebrews 11:1–3, 8–16<br>Luke 12:32–40 |
| **PROPER 15**<br>*Sunday from Aug. 14—Aug. 20* | Isaiah 56:1, 6–8<br>Psalm 67<br>Romans 11:1–2a, 29–32<br>Matthew 15:(10–20) 21–28 | Proverbs 9:1–6<br>Psalm 34:9–14<br>Ephesians 5:15–20<br>John 6:51–58 | Jeremiah 23:23–29<br>Psalm 82<br>Hebrews 11:29—12:2<br>Luke 12:49–56 |
| **PROPER 16**<br>*Sunday from Aug. 21—Aug. 27* | Isaiah 51:1–6<br>Psalm 138<br>Romans 12:1–8<br>Matthew 16:13–20 | Joshua 24:1–2a, 14–18<br>Psalm 34:15–22<br>Ephesians 6:10–20<br>John 6:56–69 | Isaiah 58:9b–14<br>Psalm 103:1–8<br>Hebrews 12:18–29<br>Luke 13:10–17 |
| **PROPER 17**<br>*Sunday from Aug. 28—Sept. 3* | Jeremiah 15:15–21<br>Psalm 26:1–8<br>Romans 12:9–21<br>Matthew 16:21–28 | Deuteronomy 4:1–2, 6–9<br>Psalm 15<br>James 1:17–27<br>Mark 7:1–8, 14–15, 21–23 | Proverbs 25:6–7<br>Psalm 112<br>Hebrews 13:1–8, 15–16<br>Luke 14:1, 7–14 |

| | YEAR A | YEAR B | YEAR C |
|---|---|---|---|
| **PROPER 18**<br>*Sunday from Sept. 4—Sept. 10* | Ezekiel 33:7–11<br>Psalm 119:33–40<br>Romans 13:8–14<br>Matthew 18:15–20 | Isaiah 35:4–7a<br>Psalm 146<br>James 2:1–10 (11–13), 14–17<br>Mark 7:24–37 | Deuteronomy 30:15–20<br>Psalm 1<br>Philemon 1–21<br>Luke 14:25–33 |
| **PROPER 19**<br>*Sunday from Sept. 11—Sept. 17* | Genesis 50:15–21<br>Psalm 103:(1–7) 8–13<br>Romans 14:1–12<br>Matthew 18:21–35 | Isaiah 50:4–9a<br>Psalm 116:1–9<br>James 3:1–12<br>Mark 8:27–38 | Exodus 32:7–14<br>Psalm 51:1–10<br>1 Timothy 1:12–17<br>Luke 15:1–10 |
| **PROPER 20**<br>*Sunday from Sept. 18—Sept. 24* | Jonah 3:10—4:11<br>Psalm 145:1–8<br>Philippians 1:21–30<br>Matthew 20:1–16 | Jeremiah 11:18–20<br>Psalm 54<br>James 3:13—4:3, 7–8a<br>Mark 9:30–37 | Amos 8:4–7<br>Psalm 113<br>1 Timothy 2:1–7<br>Luke 16:1–13 |
| **PROPER 21**<br>*Sunday from Sept. 25—Oct. 1* | Ezekiel 18:1–4, 25–32<br>Psalm 25:1–9<br>Philippians 2:1–13<br>Matthew 21:23–32 | Numbers 11:4–6, 10–16, 24–29<br>Psalm 19:7–14<br>James 5:13–20<br>Mark 9:38–50 | Amos 6:1a, 4–7<br>Psalm 146<br>1 Timothy 6:6–19<br>Luke 16:19–31 |

## WORLD COMMUNION SUNDAY

*First Sunday in October (no specific texts assigned; use Proper 21 or 22 depending on the Sunday)*

| | YEAR A | YEAR B | YEAR C |
|---|---|---|---|
| **PROPER 22**<br>*Sunday from Oct. 2—Oct. 8* | Isaiah 5:1–7<br>Psalm 80:7–15<br>Philippians 3:4b–14<br>Matthew 21:33–46 | Genesis 2:18–24<br>Psalm 8<br>Hebrews 1:1–4; 2:5–12<br>Mark 10:2–16 | Habbakuk 1:1–4, 2:1–4<br>Psalm 37:1–9<br>2 Timothy 1:1–14<br>Luke 17:5–10 |
| **PROPER 23**<br>*Sunday from Oct. 9—Oct. 15* | Isaiah 25:1–9<br>Psalm 23<br>Philippians 4:1–9<br>Matthew 22:1–14 | Amos 5:6–7, 10–15<br>Psalm 90:12–17<br>Hebrews 4:12–16<br>Mark 10:17–31 | 2 Kings 5:1–3, 7–15c<br>Psalm 111<br>2 Timothy 2:8–15<br>Luke 17:11–19 |
| **PROPER 24**<br>*Sunday from Oct. 16—Oct. 22* | Isaiah 45:1–7<br>Psalm 96:1–9 (10–13)<br>1 Thessalonians 1:1–10<br>Matthew 22:15–22 | Isaiah 53:4–12<br>Psalm 91:9–16<br>Hebrews 5:1–10<br>Mark 10:35–45 | Genesis 32:22–31<br>Psalm 121<br>2 Timothy 3:14—4:5<br>Luke 18:1–8 |

| | YEAR A | YEAR B | YEAR C |
|---|---|---|---|
| **PROPER 25** *Sunday from Oct. 23—Oct. 29* | Leviticus 19:1–2, 15–18<br>Psalm 1<br>1 Thessalonians 2:1–8<br>Matthew 22:34–46 | Jeremiah 31:7–9<br>Psalm 126<br>Hebrews 7:23–28<br>Mark 10:46–52 | Jeremiah 14:7–10, 19–22<br>Psalm 84:1–7<br>2 Timothy 4:6–8, 16–18<br>Luke 18:9–14 |
| **PROPER 26** *Sunday from Oct. 30—Nov. 5* | Micah 3:5–12<br>Psalm 43<br>1 Thessalonians 2:9–13<br>Matthew 23:1–12 | Deuteronomy 6:1–9<br>Psalm 119:1–8<br>Hebrews 9:11–14<br>Mark 12:28–34 | Isaiah 1:10–18<br>Psalm 32:1–7<br>2 Thessalonians 1:1–4, 11–12<br>Luke 19:1–10 |
| **ALL SAINTS' SUNDAY** *(can replace Proper 26 or 27 depending on the Sunday)* | | | |
| *Sunday from Nov. 1—Nov. 7* | Revelation 7:9–17<br>Psalm 34:1–10, 22<br>1 John 3:1–3<br>Matthew 5:1–12 | Isaiah 25:6–9<br>Psalm 24<br>Revelation 21:1–6a<br>John 11:32–44 | Daniel 7:1–3, 15–18<br>Psalm 149<br>Ephesians 1:11–23<br>Luke 6:20–31 |
| **PROPER 27** *Sunday from Nov. 6—Nov. 12* | Amos 5:18–24<br>Psalm 70<br>1 Thessalonians 4:13–18<br>Matthew 25:1–13 | 1 Kings 17:8–16<br>Psalm 146<br>Hebrews 9:24–28<br>Mark 12:38–44 | Job 19:23–27a<br>Psalm 17:1–9<br>2 Thessalonians 2:1–5, 13–17<br>Luke 20:27–38 |
| **PROPER 28** *Sunday from Nov. 13—Nov. 19* | Zephaniah 1:7, 12–18<br>Psalm 90:1–8 (9–11), 12<br>1 Thessalonians 5:1–11<br>Matthew 25:14–30 | Daniel 12:1–3<br>Psalm 16<br>Hebrews 10:11–14 (15–18), 19–25<br>Mark 13:1–8 | Malachi 4:1–2a<br>Psalm 98<br>2 Thessalonians 3:6–13<br>Luke 21:5–19 |
| **CHRIST THE KING SUNDAY** *(the last Sunday of the Christian Year)* | | | |
| **PROPER 29** *Sunday from Nov. 20—Nov. 26* | Ezekiel 34:11–16, 20–24<br>Psalm 95:1–7a<br>Ephesians 1:15–23<br>Matthew 25:31–46 | Daniel 7:9–10, 13–14<br>Psalm 93<br>Revelation 1:4b–8<br>John 18:33–37 | Jeremiah 23:1–6<br>Psalm 46<br>Colossians 1:11–20<br>Luke 23:33–43 |

As you can tell from the length of the list above, Ordinary Time is the longest season of the Christian Year. It is celebrated for close to half the year. In this sense, the Christian Year puts great weight on the role of the church in the story of God. Christ's life on earth is remembered for half the year, and the life of Christ lived out by the church is commemorated the rest of the year.

Another reason the season is titled "Ordinary" is because it is "ordered" time, referring to ordinal numbers—first, second, third, and so on. This is in contrast to cardinal numbers—one, two, three, and so on—which are quantitative. Unlike other seasons that associate texts to a particular week in the season counting by Sundays (for example, "The Third Sunday in Advent" or "The Eighth Sunday of Easter"), the lectionary texts in Ordinary Time are assigned to what is called a "Proper." Propers are simply services (or "Proper Liturgies") assigned to particular time frames. They are the means of keeping track of where we are in Ordinary Time without having to count all the Sundays (since we'd be counting for a bit). Remember, Ordinary Time is the longest season in the Christian Year. Rarely does Ordinary Time begin with Proper 1. The Sunday following Pentecost Sunday is always **Trinity Sunday** and the Propers pick up from there. So, if the Sunday following Trinity Sunday was June 23, you would begin by using the texts assigned to Proper 7.

The color of the season is green, as it is a season of life and growth. Ordinary Time is to the church as Epiphany is to Christ. Just as Jesus "grew in wisdom and in stature and in favor with God and all the people" in Epiphany (Luke 2:52), in Ordinary Time the church's love grows "more and more in knowledge and depth of insight, so that [we] may be able to discern what is best and may be pure and blameless for the day of Christ, filled with the fruit of righteousness that comes through Jesus Christ—to the glory and praise of God" (see Phil. 1:9–11 NIV).

The lectionary texts provided in this chapter offer Old Testament texts and Psalms that are complementary to the New Testament readings. There are, however, alternate Old Testament texts in the Revised Common Lectionary which offer a retelling of the Old Testament stories over the course of Years A, B, and C. These start in Genesis in Year A and end with the Prophets in Year C. These alternate texts are not included here simply because I assumed that if your context wasn't already using the lectionary, a three-year commitment to journeying through the Old Testament might be a big leap. But, it is certainly appropriate in Ordinary Time to journey through a book of the Bible or specific Old Testament narratives. If you choose to do this, a reverse lectionary can provide the associated references to your selected text.[2]

Heritage is important in this season. Just as you might show your children pictures in a family photo album to remember family vacations, friends, their grandparents, and their great-grandparents, Ordinary Time offers the church the opportunity to look back into our "photo album" and remember our story. We see Adam and Eve, Abraham and Sarah, Moses, Naomi, Ruth, and Esther. We remember Peter, James, and John; Paul, Lydia, and Junia; Priscilla and Aquila—and the stories go on and on. We gain an identity in remembering our heritage and in remembering God's work throughout these times. We might even catch preludes of Christ in some of the Old Testament stories after having just walked with him more closely through the first half of the year.

## WAYS TO JOIN THE COMMITMENT OF ORDINARY TIME

### REMEMBER

Remember the story of God, from Adam and Eve to the second coming of Christ. Acknowledge that we are not just onlookers to this story, but that we are invited into it! Use Old Testament stories to preach on God's faithfulness or some other specific theme. Follow Peter's ministry or Paul's missionary journeys. Focus on one character throughout a series or use the list of the faithful in Hebrews 11 to help form a schedule of stories to tell. If a preaching schedule is already in place, use the gathering portion of the service to remember these narratives. Use these stories to proclaim who God is in your call to worship, the Prayers of the People, the words between songs, or even within songs. Consider, for example, singing a song about the faithfulness of God, but introducing the song by telling the story of the Israelites' exodus from Egypt. The people are finally freed from the Egyptians, and God leads them to a dead end. Not only this, but Pharaoh changes his mind and pursues the Israelites.

> As Pharaoh approached, the people of Israel looked up and panicked when they saw the Egyptians overtaking them. . . . Moses told the people, "Do not be afraid. Just stand still and watch the LORD rescue you today. The Egyptians you see today will never be seen again. The LORD himself will fight for you. Just stay calm." Then the LORD said to Moses, ". . . Tell the people to get moving! Pick up your staff and raise your hand over the sea. Divide the water so the Israelites can walk through the middle of the sea on dry ground . . . [then] all Egypt will see my glory and know that I am the LORD!"
>
> —Exodus 14:10, 13–18

By including this story, you are not only remembering a fundamental narrative of biblical history with your congregation, but you are inviting them to reenact it. In a sense, you're welcoming your people to stand with the Israelites at the edge of the Red Sea and at the same time acknowledging that the God that split the sea is the same God leading your people out of bondage today. In either perspective, you've called attention to the fact that one thing is always true—past, present, and future—our God is a God of salvation.

Embrace the story of God and his people throughout this season. Be creative in how you remember and reenact this epic, and even ordinary, narrative. These stories are foundational to a right understanding of God and even a right understanding of ourselves. In this season of Ordinary Time, we're invited to intentionally look back to the beginning—it might actually reveal more clearly where we're at and where we're going.

## STOP NAVEL-GAZING

I had a friend in college that would repeatedly use the phrase, "Stop navel-gazing." It was his way of telling me that I needed to stop looking at myself—my own belly button—and look up and see the world. Whenever we identify a problem in our life, we often become absorbed by it. Like a pimple on our forehead, it's all we can see, and it's all we think people are seeing when they look at us. We make decisions, act, and feel out of our magnified awareness that we have a pimple on our forehead. In these "navel-gazing" times of our life, we are prone to run into even more hazards because we're so concerned about our own realities. Look up! Stop magnifying your own belly button for a season and consider what the community is doing and how you can best aid in the work of Christ alongside your brothers and sisters. Rarely does God heal us in isolation, but perhaps as we offer ourselves as instruments of grace to those around us, we will realize some of that grace was imparted to us. For grace is never for the individual as much as it is for the betterment of the whole community.

Ordinary Time reminds us of our corporate nature: our life is for the life of Christ and the church. So, include in your liturgy things that emphasize the corporate nature of the church. Have a *group* of people present the Scripture instead of *one* person. Celebrate your small groups. Offer a membership course to your congregation and celebrate the reception of members. Again, baptism and the Eucharist are primary elements that reveal our participation in Christ's work and our participation in the church universal. Embrace the ecumenical church—invite guest speakers, embrace other cultural expressions of worship, and go on cross-cultural trips. Ordinary Time invites us to let go of "how we've always done it" and "what I like" to embrace a church that existed before us and will continue to exist after us.

## SPECIAL SERVICES

### TRINITY SUNDAY

Ordinary Time does not include any prescribed special services, but it contains a number of special Sundays. I have included some of the most common special services and even one that was added by the evangelical church within the last century. The first special Sunday is actually the first Sunday of the season: Trinity Sunday. No matter the date, Trinity Sunday is always the Sunday following Pentecost and then the Propers start in order from there. Now, it must be said that every Sunday should be Trinitarian. No work of the Father, Son, or Spirit can be fully separated from the work of the other persons. However, it is on this day that the unity, distinguishability, and equality of the Father, Son, and Spirit are given more attention than usual. This could be presented by the content of songs, the creative use of harmony (i.e., the triad of a chord), the unification of diverse instruments around one single melody, the synchronization and individual interpretation of dance, the use of multiple languages (don't forget sign language), or fine art. The Russian painter, Andrei Rublev, offers a historic depiction of the Trinity gathered around one table. Perhaps you could create your own artistic expression of the unity and equality of the three while displaying the distinguishability within the one.

## WORLD COMMUNION SUNDAY

The special days slow for a couple months, but on the first Sunday of October many churches will celebrate World Communion Sunday. This day is a fairly recent evangelical addition to the festivals of the church. World Communion Sunday encapsulates the ecumenical nature of the season of Ordinary Time. Churches all around the world commit to partaking in the Eucharist on this day, approaching the table with the awareness that we are eating from a table that is open to all people, all nations, all tribes, and all languages. What a great day to sing in other languages, offer breads from around the world, and include the global church in your local context. Perhaps your congregation includes underrepresented cultures. Sit down with these people and ask them how you might insert elements unique to their heritage in corporate worship. Invite them to participate in creating, facilitating, or teaching your congregation about this form of worship.

In addition to those that directly represent a culture different than your own, look for culture in places you wouldn't expect to find it. Culture transcends skin color, race, and time. Brainstorm ways to encourage families to look beyond their current reality to embrace their own family heritage. They might just discover more culture than they thought they ever had.

In my context, there are eight Communion "stations" at which a pair of people administer the sacrament to a particular section of people in the sanctuary. On World Communion Sunday, we ask families to adopt one of these stations and encourage them to research their family history and then build or decorate a Communion station representative of the culture of their heritage. As a tablecloth, they bring fabric (not a national flag) that symbolizes the cultural art of their heritage. They bring a bowl or basket as well as a chalice of some sort and bake or buy bread common to that culture. They might even learn how to say the words of administration in the language of their native culture: "The body of Christ, the bread of heaven" and "The blood of Christ, the cup of salvation" (or sometimes just "The body of Christ" and "The blood of Christ," depending on the difficulty of the language and their comfortability with it).

In my context, two families who adopted older children created stations representative of their new kids' home cultures. In an act of hospitality, these families took on the culture of their new family members. Through these practices of World Communion Sunday, our church has discovered that we are more diverse than we once thought. Not only does our congregation include people who are directly from around the world, but we've come to realize that we all come from someplace beyond what we've always known.

### ALL SAINTS' SUNDAY

All Saints' Day is commemorated on November 1, and on the Sunday following, the church commemorates All Saints' Sunday. Celebrating saints may be a stretch for many evangelical churches; however, to hopefully inspire more unity than division around this particular day, I'll aim to simplify it. The heart of this day is simply to remember and celebrate those in the faith that went before us and acknowledge their part in forming the church we know today.

Different traditions have different lists of these "saints" just as you could provide a unique list of people that have formed and shaped you throughout your lifetime. All Saints' Sunday is the day we celebrate these people.

Since there are numerous connotations of this day and perhaps even of the word *saint*, you would be wise to take care in how you commemorate this day. The day uniquely promotes the ethos of Ordinary Time by looking into the history of the church and identifying individuals that modeled commitment to Christ and his church. It truly is a beautiful day of celebration, but as with anything new, explanation, consideration, and intentionality are key.

We regularly include a choir in my context but are sure to schedule them on special Sundays in Ordinary Time and even more intentionally on All Saints' Sunday. The inclusion of a choir emphasizes the corporate ethos of the day. Seeing four times the regular number of people on the platform promotes an unavoidable corporate nature to the service. More specific to the day, however, is a time of memory for those within our congregation that have passed away in the preceding year. In the weeks before this Sunday, staff members contact families of those who have died in the previous twelve months and ask if they would like to include a photo of their family member in a slideshow that will play within the service. This is done not only to get permission but also to make the family aware that they'll see their loved one's picture projected on this day. Depending on where they are in the grieving process, this could be a difficult thing to experience publicly, if they aren't prepared for it. These calls also offer an opportunity for staff to check in on these families and ask if they are in need of anything and to offer prayer. Normally the slideshow is introduced and explained after singing a couple songs. It is then followed by a short chorus of thanksgiving or revelation of God's faithfulness, love, and abundant life.

## CHRIST THE KING SUNDAY

Just as a new year is commemorated, the final Sunday of the Christian Year is Christ the King Sunday. This day is a celebration of Christ as prophet, priest, and king of all nations. The following Sunday the Christian Year will begin again on the first Sunday of Advent. Celebrate this conclusion; it's been a long emotional journey. In considering how your context does celebration, perhaps this day will include a potluck following the service. Maybe you could offer a service of testimonies and prayer. Perhaps it's a day to simply try something new that sets the day apart from all other Sundays.

Christ the King Sunday has gone through a couple different revisions in my context. When we first began celebrating this special Sunday, we did so by including more instruments and were intentional about including songs that elevated Christ as king. More recently we've developed a Sunday morning service we call "The Christian Year Service." On this special day, we use the full service time to walk through the entire narrative of Christ's life. We begin in Advent, celebrate Christmas, Epiphany, journey to the cross in Lent, celebrate Easter, and respond to Christ at the table in Ordinary Time—all in just over an hour. We sing, we present Scripture, we pray, we light Advent candles, we change the altar cloth, we take Communion—it's a full service. In a sense, it's like the recap videos that play on New Year's Eve night. We basically collect all the elements we used throughout the previous year to walk through the Christian Year and then incorporate them all into this one service.

Whatever you decide to do on this Sunday, whether you walk through the whole story of Christ together one last time, or you create some other service or service elements, this day should elevate and glorify Christ as Lord of all. "'I am the Alpha and the Omega—the beginning and the end,' says the Lord God. 'I am the one who is, who always was, and who is still to come—the Almighty One'" (Rev. 1:8).

# TELLING CHRIST'S STORY BEYOND THE SUNDAY GATHERING

The Sunday assembly, historically referred to as "The Lord's Day," is the primary means by which we tell the story of God. "Without the weekly rhythm of creation and re-creation," writes Constance Cherry, "there is no basis for the rest of the Christian Year. The Lord's Day is the foundation of it all."[1] And yet, there are seasons when it is appropriate to offer opportunities in addition to the Lord's Day, whether activities or readings to be done throughout the week, or the inclusion of another service. In a sense, these special services give us landmarks as we journey through the Christian Year. They give special and extended attention to telling us where we've been, where we currently are, and where we're headed. And if we need a change of course, these special services offer us the right trajectory to return to God.

Also, depending on how much influence you actually have on the Sunday worship service, I have found that special services are a great means of beginning to elevate the story of Christ and introduce your congregation to new—or probably more accurately—old ways to worship (i.e., getting back to the basics of experiencing the revelation of God and responding to him). There are numerous important elements that need to be present in your weekly gathering, but special services offer a bit more freedom. The options truly are endless when it comes to creatively facilitating a service for your congregation to reenact—to *re*member (i.e., put back together)—the story of God and offer opportunities to respond to it.

In thinking back to the colors associated with each season, you may have noticed a pattern: blue/purple, white, green—and then again, purple, white, and green. Both Advent and Lent are reflective seasons represented by their darker royal color(s). Christmas and Easter are both high seasons of white, emphasizing the celebration of God's life-changing work. The green seasons—Epiphany and Ordinary Time—are seasons of growth and action.

The most common special services are associated with the seasons of Advent and Lent. They are reflective seasons meant to correct our posture in relation to God and prepare us for the seasons to follow. Christmas and Easter elevate the importance of the Lord's Day, celebrating and proclaiming the foundations of our faith: Christ's incarnation and resurrection. Epiphany and Ordinary Time exhort the ministry of the church beyond its walls.

Therefore, the special services I've included in this chapter are specific to Advent and Lent, with the exception of one special Sunday service I've provided for Christ the King Sunday—the last Sunday of the Christian Year. You are certainly invited and encouraged to create special services and opportunities beyond the ones listed here for any season, but special services are not always necessary or the most appropriate opportunity you can offer your congregation. During Christmas and Easter, I encourage you to begin by using ideas already included in this book to give special attention to *celebrating* Christ's life on the Lord's Day. In Epiphany and Ordinary Time, brainstorm in your context how you might give special attention to enacting Christ's life beyond the corporate gathering. Remember, we're following the story of the God-man; so even though he is God, we should not be surprised to find in each season the prominence of a specific human attribute: thinking and reflection in Advent and Lent, feeling and affection in Christmas and Easter, and doing and action in Epiphany and Ordinary Time.

After deciding when you want to offer a special service, next comes the actual planning. Everyone has to find their own process but sometimes having someone else's method can give you a place to start, and then you can bend and form it to create your own. So, perhaps this bird's-eye view of a planning process can offer you a place to start. Begin by gathering a small team of people in a room and discussing the four questions below. Try to get a good blend of perspectives: creative, practical, nerdy, passionate—maybe a younger kid, a stay-at-home parent, a retiree. Push yourselves to arrive at detailed answers to the following questions. There are so many different options for what any context could do. Your answers to the following questions will bring focus to the special service you're planning and give you greater freedom in shaping all the ideas you have.

1. **Fabric:** What's the content or story of this service? Read through texts assigned to the day or season. Grasp this portion of the story in relation to the greater narrative.
2. **Function:** Why are we telling this story? What does it teach us about God and our part in his story?
3. **Formation:** Who do we become as a result of remembering this story? What type of people are we hoping to form our congregation into because of this service?
4. **Form:** How do we structure this story in a way that allows our people to engage in it? Are there any historic practices that could be drawn from? Are there any specific elements, songs, or Scripture texts that should be used?

After this brainstorming session, the service in its final form probably won't come to you for a couple more days (or weeks if you're like me). You'll wrestle with Scripture texts, order of elements, the size of your space, and other practicalities. Never forget: in their simplest form, these services should primarily tell the story of God (revelation) with opportunities for your people to engage in (respond to) that story. So, never lose sight of Christ as you're planning, ask the Father for some of his creativity, and actively wait for the Holy Spirit to guide you.

In the following pages, I offer ideas for special services from past seasons that a team and I created for our context. There are already plenty of great resources being produced that outline standard special services for the church, the Discipleship Ministries of the United Methodist church being a prominent example.[2] The services you find here are perhaps less standard and a bit more interpretive than what might be considered traditional. You might find more details than you're looking for, but you'll see different ideas of how to break up the narrative, different patterns of revelation and response, the use of symbols, contrasted themes, and art. Whether you skim this chapter, or you read every word, I hope these ideas will inspire creativity on your own journey of remembering the story of God with the people of God!

## ADVENT SPECIAL SERVICES

Three special services for the season of Advent are outlined below. Depending on your current church calendar, your staffing, and available volunteers, you'll have to determine what is beneficial and possible for your people during this season. I'd suggest starting with the inclusion of a Christmas Eve service. However, if Christmas Eve is already a regular service for your context, and you're interested in a specifically Advent-themed special service, Hanging of the Greens and the O Antiphons might provide some inspiration for other opportunities to invite your people into this season of anticipation.

## HANGING OF THE GREENS

Many churches decorate their sanctuaries during the seasons of Advent and Christmas, yet rarely are those Christmas decorations considered for their symbolism in telling the story of Christ. In a Hanging of the Greens service, the sanctuary is decorated with the traditional poinsettias, wreaths, and garland, but they are placed while the story of God is told and they remain throughout the season as representations of God's story coming to fruition in Christ.

You might use the following to acknowledge God's transcendent presence: a blue altar cloth, perhaps even danced in, to celebrate the hope of a Creator that has relationship with his creation; red poinsettias to remember the suffering of God's people throughout history; a wreath and garland to reveal the ongoing hope of redemption for all creation; a nativity scene to give visible form to the birth of Christ; light to illuminate us with the prophecy of *the* Light entering the world; and ornaments on a tree to symbolize the diversity and spreading of the church throughout the world.

Christ's story can be proclaimed with more than words. After a Hanging of the Greens service, perhaps your congregation will see more than festive décor surrounding them. Perhaps they might also see the story of God. Consider the use of these common symbols:

- Sound and incense: symbolizing God's existence within the void (see Gen. 1:1–2).
- Blue altar cloth: symbolizing the hope of God's covenant (see Gen. 12:1–3 *or* 17:1–8).
- Red poinsettias: symbolizing the suffering of God's people (see Ps. 22:1–5, 15–21).
- Wreath and garland: symbolizing the promise of salvation (see Is. 40:9–11 *or* Zeph. 3:14–20).
- Crèche: symbolizing the manifestation of God with us (see Matt. 1:18–25).

- Light: symbolizing the work of Christ in the world (see John 1:1–5, 10–14).
- Ornaments: symbolizing the establishment of the church (see Matt. 28:18–20 *or* Acts 2:42–47).

## O ANTIPHONS

Similar to a Lessons and Carols service in format, this O Antiphons service focuses on each verse of the carol "O Come, O Come Emmanuel."[3] Each verse offers another name and promise of God fulfilled in Christ: Emmanuel, Wisdom, Lord of Might, Key of David, Rod of Jesse, King of Nations, and Dayspring. This service is also unique in that it considers Advent from both the perspective of the first Advent and the second Advent. The service begins with the ascension of Jesus, and the singing of each antiphon is paired with an exhortation from the New Testament and a prophecy primarily from the Old Testament.

### THE ASCENSION OF CHRIST:

| | |
|---|---|
| *Luke:* | Acts 1:6–8a |
| *Mark:* | Mark 16:15–16 |
| *Matthew:* | Matthew 28:20 |
| *Luke:* | Acts 1:9–11 |

[Congregational song praising the work of Christ on earth]

### THE PLEA OF THE PEOPLE OF GOD:

***All:*** Isaiah 64:1, 3–4: "*Oh, that you would burst from the heavens and come down . . .*"

***"O come, O Come, Emmanuel . . ."***

THE WAITING I:

*Exhortation:* James 5:7–8: "*Dear brothers and sisters, be patient as you wait for the Lord's return . . .*"

***All:*** **"O come, O Wisdom from on high . . ."**

*Prophecy:* Isaiah 40:1, 3b–5a; Malachi 3:2; Isaiah 40:9–11a: "*'Comfort, comfort my people,' says your God . . .*"

[Congregational song anticipating Christ]

THE WAITING II:

*Exhortation:* 2 Timothy 3:1–5; 4:5 "*You should know this . . . that in the last days there will be very difficult times . . .*"

***All:*** **"O come, O come, great Lord of Might . . ."**

*Prophecy:* Zephaniah 3:14–15b, 17b–19a, 20 "*Sing, O daughter of Zion; shout aloud, O Israel . . .*"

[Congregational song anticipating Christ]

THE WAITING III:

*Exhortation:* 1 Corinthians 1:7–9; Philippians 3:20–21 "*Now you have every spiritual gift you need as you eagerly wait for the return of our Lord . . .*"

***All:*** **"O come, O Key of David, come . . ."**

*Prophecy:* Isaiah 35:1–2a, 3–6, 8 "*Even the wilderness and desert will be glad . . .*"

[Congregational song anticipating Christ]

THE WAITING IV:

*Exhortation:* 2 Peter 3:3–5a, 8–10a "*Most importantly, I want to remind you that in the last days scoffers will come . . .*"

***All:*** **"O come, O Rod of Jesse . . ."**

*Prophecy:* Micah 5:2–5a "*But you, O Bethlehem Ephrathah . . .*"

[Congregational song anticipating Christ]

**THE WAITING V:**

*Exhortation:* Hebrews 10:23–25; 13:14 *"Let us hold tightly without wavering to the hope we affirm . . ."*

***All:*** ***"O come, O King of Nations . . ."***

*Prophecy:* Isaiah 9:2, 4a, 6–7 *"The people who walk in darkness will see a great light . . ."*

[Congregational song anticipating Christ]

**THE REVELATION:**

***All:*** ***"O come, thou Dayspring . . ."***

*Exhortation:* Revelation 22:12–13, 20a *"Look, I am coming soon . . ."*

***All:*** ***"Rejoice! Rejoice! . . ."***

*Prophecy:* Luke 1:26b–35, 37 *"God sent the angel Gabriel to Nazareth . . ."*

[Congregational song celebrating Christ's coming]

## CHRISTMAS EVE

For kids and adults alike, Christmas Eve is filled with anticipation and excitement for what's about to come. In this special service, the corporate gathering feels more like a family living room, as the congregation is invited to literally enact the building of the narrative through a series of Scriptures and carols, culminating with a candle lighting ceremony. As mentioned in the Advent chapter, many traditions don't offer a Christmas Day service, so this service may act as a welcoming and a celebration of the "true light, who gives light to everyone" (John 1:9).

Have a room full of nativity costumes, and invite families to come a few minutes early for their kids to choose a character before the service begins (cattle, donkeys, angels, shepherds, and magi). You might want to hand pick your Mary and Joseph since they have a rather prominent role. It might be wise to ask a couple older youth or adults to dress up and be the designated leaders of the cattle, angels, magi, etc. Then, instruct the families to look for their child's cue (whether on a screen or in a bulletin) to come forward and take their place in the nativity. The service is in two parts: the first being the rising tension of a need for a Savior and the second being the falling action upon recognizing the Savior has come. See an outline of the service below:

**Creation Account:** Consider an artful interpretation of the creation account: dance, paraphrase translation (even consider a children's Bible), fine art, etc.[4] For the following idea, I've assumed the inclusion of the characters of Adam and Eve.

**The Fall:** Present Genesis 3:1–6, perhaps with Adam and Eve taking hold of a large black or gray cloth to symbolize the entrance of sin into the world. In addition to this, consider the metanarrative implications of the fall in the lives of Cain, Sarai, Rebekah, and the brothers of Joseph (Judah)—each coming forward and taking hold of (even getting tangled up in) the same cloth. See the following example:

| | |
|---|---|
| *Narrator:* | [Read Gen. 3:1–6: *Adam and Eve are convinced by the serpent and eat the fruit.*] |
| *Cain:* | I told my brother Abel, "Let's go out into the fields." And while we were there, I attacked him and killed him (see Gen. 4:8). |
| *Sarai:* | I, and my husband Abram, tried to do God's work on our own and we exploited and abused my servant Hagar in the process (see Gen. 16:1–6). |
| *Rebekah:* | I helped my son Jacob deceive his father to receive his brother's inheritance (see Gen. 25:28; 27:1–40). |
| *Judah:* | My brothers and I hated our younger brother Joseph and we sold him to slave traders (see Gen. 37:4, 18–28). |

*Narrator:* [Read Gen. 3:8–19: *God discovers what Adam and Eve have done and explains what will happen to their life as a result.*]

**Prophecies of a Savior:** In turn, each of the above characters could drop their hold of the cloth and take hold instead of one of the Advent candles. Consider using the verses of "O Come, O Come, Emmanuel" as a congregational response to each prophecy. See the following example:

**[Instrumental verse of "O Come, O Come, Emmanuel"]**

*Cain:* *Takes hold of/lights the first Advent candle (blue/purple) and presents* Isaiah 64:1, 3–4 *"Oh, that you would burst from the heavens and come down . . ."*

***All:*** ***"O come, O come, Emmanuel . . ."***

*Sarai:* *Takes hold of/lights the second Advent candle (blue/purple) and presents* Isaiah 40:1–2a, 3, 5 *"'Comfort, comfort my people,' says your God . . ."*

***All:*** ***"O come, thou Rod of Jesse . . ."***

*Rebekah:* *Takes hold of/lights the third Advent candle (pink) and presents* Isaiah 40:9c–11 *"Tell the towns of Judah, 'Your God is coming!' . . ."*

***All:*** ***"O come, thou Wisdom . . ."***

*Judah:* *Takes hold of/lights the fourth Advent candle (blue/purple) and presents* Micah 5:2–5a *"But you, O Bethlehem Ephrathah . . ."*

***All:*** ***"O come, Desire of Nations . . ."***

*Adam and Eve together take hold of/light the Christ candle (white)*

*Narrator:* Luke 1:26b–35, 37–38 *"God sent the angel Gabriel to Nazareth . . ."*

***All:*** **"*Rejoice! Rejoice! Emmanuel . . .*"**
*Candles are placed, lit, in the Advent wreath.*
[Explanation and invitation to build the living nativity]

**Nativity Movement I:** *Consider using multiple readers to include more of your congregation in this service.*

*Reader 1:* Luke 2:1, 3–5 *"At that time the Roman emperor . . ."*
*Mary, Joseph, and baby Jesus are instructed via screen or bulletin to move into place as the congregation sings.*
[Suggested congregational song: "O Little Town of Bethlehem"]

**Nativity Movement II:**
*Reader 2:* Luke 2:6–7 *"And while they were there, the time came . . ."*
*The cattle and donkeys are instructed to move into place as the congregation sings.*
[Suggested congregational song: "Away in a Manger"]

**Nativity Movement III:**
*Reader 3:* Luke 2:8–14 *"That night there were shepherds . . ."*
*The angels are instructed to move into place as the congregation sings.*
[Suggested congregational song: "Angels We Have Heard on High"]

**Nativity Movement IV:**
*Reader 4:* Luke 2:15–20 *"When the angels had returned to heaven . . ."*
*The shepherds are instructed to move into place as the congregation sings.*
[Suggested congregational song: "Go Tell It on the Mountain"]

**Nativity Movement V:**

*Reader 5:* Matthew 2:1b–12 *"About that time some wise men . . ."*
*The magi are instructed to move into place as the congregation sings.*

[Suggested congregational song: "What Child Is This?"]

**Lighting of the Candles:** If you would like to end your Christmas Eve service with a candle lighting ceremony, perhaps you could pass out candles as people first arrive or set out baskets for people to grab their own as they enter the sanctuary.

[Explanation and instructions for congregational candle lighting]

While the congregation stands and sings the final song, have ushers receive light from the Christ candle and then share the light with the first person in each row, who in turn will share the light with the rest of their row.

[Suggested congregational song: "Silent Night"]

**Benediction:** Give a scriptural blessing to the congregation as you send them out to be God's light in a dark world.

## LENTEN SPECIAL SERVICES

Numerous special service samples for the season of Lent are included in the following pages: an Ash Wednesday service, the beginning of a Palm Sunday morning service, vesper services for Holy Week, as well as multiple Good Friday services.

## ASH WEDNESDAY

In this interpretation of an Ash Wednesday service, we witness the creation of the world by the triune God—Father, Son, and Holy Spirit—the fall, and the fall's effect. We confess our part in the fall, and God speaks to us through the prophet Isaiah to enact our faith in our lives. Then the Lord invites us to his table to be nourished before sending us out to feed a hungry world. This service is unique in that there is no written sermon but only the creative presentation of Scripture as the Word portion.

### *Gathering*

[Call to Worship and Invocation]

[Congregational song of revelation]

**Creation and the Fall:**

| | |
|---|---|
| *Narrator:* | Remember this portion of the story of God:<br>*Three people representing the Holy Trinity process into the sanctuary singing in three-part harmony (a progression or song with or without words).*<br><br>Then God said, |
| *Father:* | Genesis 1:26 *"Let us make human beings in our image . . ."* |
| *Narrator:* | Genesis 1:27–28a *"So God created human beings . . ."* |
| *Holy Spirit:* | Genesis 1:28b *"Be fruitful and multiply . . ."* |
| *Narrator:* | Then God said, |
| *Son:* | Genesis 1:29–30a *"Look! I have given you . . ."* |
| *Narrator:* | Genesis 1:30b–2:4, 2:15–16a *"And that is what happened . . ."* |
| *Son:* | Genesis 2:16b *"You may freely eat the fruit of every tree . . ."* |

*Holy Spirit:* Genesis 2:17a *". . . except the tree of the knowledge of good and evil."*

*Father:* Genesis 2:17b *"If you eat its fruit, you are sure to die."*

*In turn, five congregation members stand in their place and shout:*

You won't die! (see Gen. 3:4a).

*Five congregants then sit.*

*Narrator:* Genesis 3:6 *"The woman was convinced . . ."*

[Congregational song of response asking for the Lord's mercy]

**The Effects of the Fall:**

*Father:* Isaiah 24:4–6a *"The earth mourns and dries up . . ."*

*Son:* Isaiah 24:7–9 *"The grapevines waste away . . ."*

*Holy Spirit:* Isaiah 24:10–13 *"The city writhes in chaos . . ."*

[Consider reprising the same congregational song above.]

[Consider with great care the possibility of including here elements revealing contemporary effects of the fall (recent imagery of devastation, testimonies, etc.)]

*Narrator:* Romans 8:20–23 *"Against its will, all creation was subjected to God's curse . . ."*

[Consider reprising the same congregational song above before continuing on to a congregational song praising the holiness of God.]

**The Imposition of Ashes:**

[Ash Wednesday Prayer: *Consider writing your own prayer or using the collect assigned to Ash Wednesday from the Book of Common Prayer seen on the next page.*]

> Almighty and everlasting God, you hate nothing you have made and forgive the sins of all who are penitent: Create and make in us new and contrite hearts, that we, worthily lamenting our sins and acknowledging our wretchedness, may obtain of you, the God of all mercy, perfect remission and forgiveness; through Jesus Christ our Lord, who lives and reigns with you and the Holy Spirit, one God, for ever and ever. *Amen.*[5]

[Explanation and invitation to ashing]
[Imposition of ashes]

***Word***

**Old Testament Lesson:** *The "Trinity," sitting around the Communion table, present Isaiah 58:1–12, 14b. Notice all three persons will speak together when lines are assigned to "God," and the people have lines as well.*

| | |
|---|---|
| *Son:* | Shout with the voice of a trumpet blast. |
| *Father:* | Shout aloud! Don't be timid. |
| *Holy Spirit:* | Tell my people Israel of their sins! |
| *Father:* | Yet they act so pious! |
| *Son:* | They come to the Temple every day and seem delighted to learn all about me. |
| *Holy Spirit:* | They act like a righteous nation that would never abandon the laws of its God. |
| *Father:* | They ask me to take action on their behalf, pretending they want to be near me. |
| *Son:* | They say, |

| | |
|---|---|
| *People:* | We have fasted before you! Why aren't you impressed? We have been very hard on ourselves, and you don't even notice it! |
| *God:* | I will tell you why! |
| *Father:* | It's because you are fasting to please yourselves. |
| *Son:* | Even while you fast, you keep oppressing your workers. |
| *Holy Spirit:* | What good is fasting when you keep on fighting and quarreling? |
| *Father:* | This kind of fasting will never get you anywhere with me. |
| *Son:* | You humble yourselves by going through the motions of penance, bowing your heads like reeds bending in the wind. |
| *Holy Spirit :* | You dress in burlap and cover your whole body with ashes. |
| *Father:* | Is this what you call fasting? |
| *Son:* | Do you really think this will please the Lord? |
| *God:* | No! |
| *Father:* | This is the kind of fasting I want: |
| *Son:* | Free those who are wrongly imprisoned; |
| *Holy Spirit:* | lighten the burden of those who work for you. |
| *God:* | Let the oppressed go free, |
| *Holy Spirit:* | and remove the chains that bind people. |
| *Son:* | Share your food with the hungry, |
| *Holy Spirit:* | and give shelter to the homeless. |
| *Father:* | Give clothes to those who need them, |
| *Holy Spirit:* | and do not hide from relatives who need your help. |
| *Son:* | Then your salvation will come like the dawn, and your wounds will quickly heal. |
| *Father:* | Your godliness will lead you forward, |
| *Holy Spirit:* | and the glory of the Lord will protect you from behind. |

*Father:* Then when you call,
*Son:* the Lord will quickly answer.
*God:* "Yes, I am here,"
*Holy Spirit :* Remove the heavy yoke of oppression.
*Father:* Stop pointing your finger and spreading vicious rumors!
*Son:* Feed the hungry, and help those in trouble.
*Holy Spirit:* Then your light will shine out from the darkness,
*Father:* and the darkness around you will be as bright as noon.
*Son:* The Lord will guide you continually, giving you water when you are dry and restoring your strength.
*Father:* You will be like a well-watered garden, like an ever-flowing spring.
*Holy Spirit:* Some of you will rebuild the deserted ruins of your cities. Then you will be known as a rebuilder of walls and a restorer of homes.
*God:* I, the Lord, have spoken!

**Psalm:** *The same five congregation members who shouted Genesis 3:4a, in turn now stand and proclaim Psalm 51:1–17:*

1. Psalm 51:1–3 *"Have mercy on me, O God . . ."*
2. Psalm 51:4–6 *"Against you, and you alone, have I sinned . . ."*
3. Psalm 51:7–11 *"Purify me from my sins . . ."*
4. Psalm 51:12–15 *"Restore to me the joy of your salvation . . ."*
5. Psalm 51:16–17 *"You do not desire a sacrifice . . ."*

**Epistle:** *Presented by a pastor, taking into consideration any current sufferings of the congregation and transposing them within chapter 6, verses 8 and 9 of the reading.*
2 Corinthians 5:20b—6:10 *"Come back to God!"*

**Response to the Word:**
[Prayer of Confession]
[Assurance of Pardon]
[Congregational song of praise in response to God's mercy]

***Table***

[Eucharistic Prayer: *(1) Thank God for his work of salvation epitomized in Christ. (2) Remember Christ's words when he took bread, blessed it, broke it, and gave it (see Matt. 26:26–28; Mark 14:22–24; Luke 22:19–20 or 24:30; John 6:11). (3) Ask the Holy Spirit to bless the elements.*]
[Invitation to the Table]
[Communion]

***Sending***

[Post-Communion Prayer: *Thank God for his sustenance and assurance that we are part of the body of Christ. Ask him to send us out to continue his work in the communities we are a part of.*]
Isaiah 58:6b–7—*"Free those who are wrongly imprisoned . . ."*
[Benediction: *Give a scriptural blessing to the congregation as you send them out to feed a hungry world.*]

## PALM SUNDAY

Palm Sunday offers a great opportunity to intermix Scripture and song in retelling the triumphal entry as well as foreshadowing the events about to take place in Holy Week. The following is a proposed order for just the beginning of the gathering portion of the service. This also offers an example of including the story of Christ even when you don't have access to planning the whole service. Texts are assigned to a leader, a chorus of people, and to *All*.

**Call to Worship:** *Psalm 118:1*

*Leader:* Give thanks to the LORD, for he is good!

***All:*** **His faithful love endures forever.**

**Invocation:** *Transposed from Psalm 118:*

*Leader:* LORD, our cornerstone,
you are our strength and our song.
Open up the gates that lead to your presence,
so we may enter and give thanks to the LORD.
You are our God, and we will praise you!
You are our God, and we will exalt you!

[Congregational song of praise to Christ]

**The Triumphal Entry:**

*Leader:* John 12:12–13a *"The news that Jesus was on the way to Jerusalem swept through the city . . ."*

*Chorus randomly shouts:*

Praise God!
Blessings on the one who comes in the name of the LORD.
Hail to the King of Israel!

[Congregational song voicing "Hosanna"]

*Kids enter sanctuary, waving palm branches, journey throughout the room for the duration of the song, and then stop upon the continuation of the text.*

*Leader:* But some of the Pharisees among the crowd said,
*Chorus:* Teacher, rebuke your followers!
*Leader:* He replied, "If they kept quiet, the stones along the road would burst into cheers!"

But as he came closer to Jerusalem and saw the city ahead, he began to weep. "How I wish today that you of all people would understand the way to peace. But now it is too late, and peace is hidden from your eyes, [for] you did not recognize it when God visited you (see Luke 19:39–42, 44b).

[Later, Jesus told the crowd,] "My light will shine for you just a little longer. Walk in the light while you can, so the darkness will not overtake you" (John 12:35a).

**[Congregational song that alludes to the cross]**

*Continue your regular service order.*

## VESPER SERVICES

For many people, Holy Week is just another week in the year. We may have plans for an extended Easter weekend with family, but not much else breaks our regular routine. However, this holy weekend—traditionally called the "Triduum" (*trid*-oo-um), meaning "three days" in Latin—is not just an ordinary weekend. There is a betrayal (see Mark 14:10), a desertion (see Mark 14:50), a scandal of a trial (see Mark 14:57), a suicide (see Matt. 27:5), excessive force and humiliation (see Mark 15:16–20), a public death (see John 19:30), an earthquake (see Matt. 27:51), godly zombies (see Matt. 27:52), a funeral (see John 19:40), a burial (see John 19:42), and somehow at the end of it all, a resurrection (see Mark 16:6). I'm not sure what your life looks like, but this is not my definition of an ordinary weekend! I need a little time to prepare for all of this.

Holy Week offers the opportunity to remember the entirety of the final week before Christ's death. Of any week in the Christian Year, it seems appropriate to journey with Jesus one day at a time. Vespers services provide this space to remember, pray, and give thanks. These services can be rather simple and follow the same order each day, only exchanging the sung refrain, prayer, and assigned daily lectionary readings (see the Lenten chapter for these texts). In my context, we hold these thirty-minute services in a smaller chapel area at 5:30 p.m. This allows people to come to the service straight from work and still have dinner shortly after 6:00. You'll see a basic layout of a proposed vespers service below and an alternate rendition following.

**Gathering:**
[Call to Worship]
[Invocation]
[Sung Refrain]

**Word:**
[Old Testament Lesson]
[Psalm: *Consider formatting the psalm as a responsive reading, or find sung refrains associated to each daily psalm*]
[Gospel Reading]
[Prayers of the People: *If it's a smaller setting, consider including bidding prayers in which a leader offers prompts for the people to speak aloud their prayers (e.g., "Lord, we lift up the names of those that need your healing power . . .")*]
[The Lord's Prayer]

**Table:**
[Eucharistic Prayer: *(1) Thank God for his work of salvation epitomized in Christ. (2) Remember Christ's words when he took bread, blessed it, broke it, and gave it (see Matt. 26:26–28; Mark 14:22–24; Luke*

*22:19–20 or 24:30; John 6:11). (3) Ask the Holy Spirit to bless the elements.*]
[Invitation to the Table]
[Communion]

**Sending:**
[Post-Communion Prayer: *Thank God for his sustenance and assurance that we are part of the body of Christ. Ask him to send us out to continue his work in the communities we are a part of.*]
[Benediction: *Give a scriptural blessing to the congregation as you send them out to be food for a hungry world. Consider using language from the assigned daily epistle.*]

The above offers a rather straightforward approach to the events of Holy Week. Below, you'll find an alternative approach to Holy Week which offers a more expositional or even metaphorical approach to the week. Each service still includes the narrative of Christ's journey to the cross, which I would suggest placing after the opening sung refrain and then reprising that refrain after. The assigned texts for the Word portion then offer an explanation to what Christ is doing in offering himself to death.

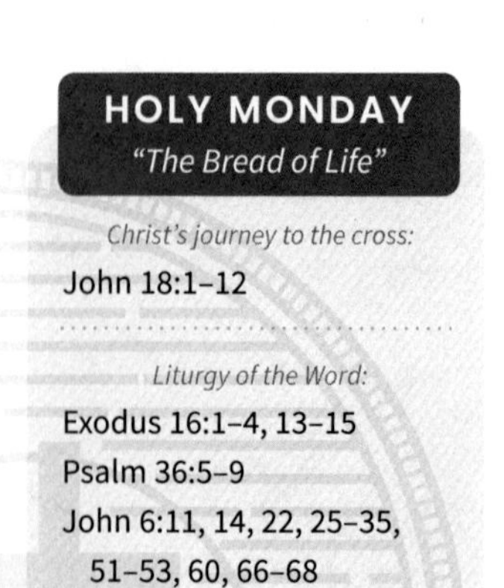

**HOLY MONDAY**
*"The Bread of Life"*

*Christ's journey to the cross:*
John 18:1–12

*Liturgy of the Word:*
Exodus 16:1–4, 13–15
Psalm 36:5–9
John 6:11, 14, 22, 25–35, 51–53, 60, 66–68

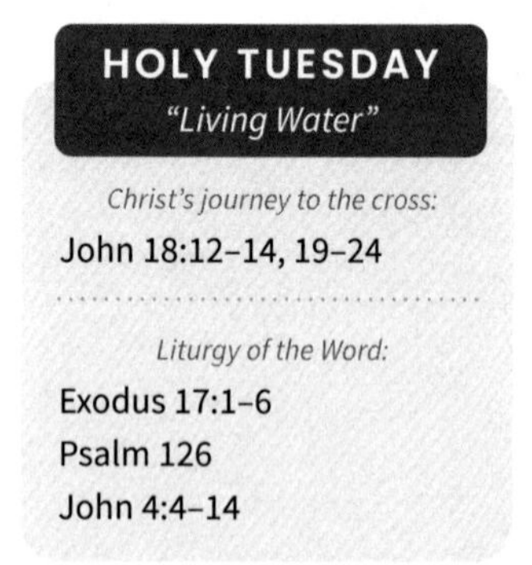

**HOLY TUESDAY**
*"Living Water"*

*Christ's journey to the cross:*
John 18:12–14, 19–24

*Liturgy of the Word:*
Exodus 17:1–6
Psalm 126
John 4:4–14

**HOLY WEDNESDAY**
*"The Good Shepherd"*

*Christ's journey to the cross:*
John 18:28–40

*Liturgy of the Word:*
Jeremiah 23:1–6
Psalm 23
John 10:11–21

**HOLY THURSDAY**
*"The True Vine"*

*Christ's journey to the cross:*
John 19:1–16

*Liturgy of the Word:*
Isaiah 5:1–7
Psalm 80
John 15:1–15

You'll find four more examples of Good Friday services in the pages to follow, each with its own unique qualities. But if you offered Holy Week vespers services and used the alternate texts above, then let me offer texts for a Good Friday service that continue in the same vein of narrative, metaphor, and exposition. Below you'll find a suggested order by which to present these Scriptures, recognizing that you would include other elements in your service to allow the congregation to participate and respond in the liturgy. I'd suggest not partaking of Communion in this service and instead including the additional texts. Begin with the foreshadowing of Christ, then move to the liturgy of the Word, and then conclude with Christ's journey to the cross and the exposition from the epistle. If it is appropriate for your context, this service would lend itself to the Veneration of the Cross.

**GOOD FRIDAY**

*"The Bronze Serpent"*

1. *Foreshadowing of Christ:*
   Numbers 11:4–9, 21:4–9

2. *Liturgy of the Word:*
   Deuteronomy 8:10–18
   Psalm 31:1–5
   John 3:1–18

   *Additional texts:*
   John 8:12–16, 19, 23–28
   John 12:20–33

3. *Christ's journey to the cross:*
   John 19:17–30

   *Exposition:*
   1 Corinthians 10:1–6, 9–13

## GOOD FRIDAY: CONTRAST

Though the instructions of the following service are minimal, the texts offer a juxtaposition of Christ being the "true light" (John 1:9) against the darkening narrative of his death. The narrative of Christ's journey to the cross moves chronologically while the revelation of Christ as light moves in reverse chronological order. The overarching contrast is that as the crucifixion narrative seems to be getting darker and darker (literally too, as candles are extinguished in each scene), the "light" narrative is making bolder and bolder claims of Christ's supremacy over darkness. Therefore, the congregation joins the confusion of Christ's followers as they see the Light of the World succumb to the darkness of death.

I encourage you to explore the different ways these texts could be presented beyond just reading them. Explore the art of underscoring—using instruments to represent different characters within the crucifixion narrative. Practice different ways you might present the light texts using the art of tableau. Perhaps two artists could paint during the readings—one using a white canvas with black paint during the crucifixion narrative and the other using a black canvas with white paint during the light texts. Consider those in your context and seek to utilize their skills in presenting these contrasting perspectives.

Notice that in this service and the following two, I've included optional times for congregational response, whether it be by singing, reciting a litany, or another action. These are optional only in the sense that you might not include a response after every scene, but rather after only a few. Your service *should* include opportunities for response; I've simply left it up to you to be intentional in your context with when and how you do this.

**Prophecies of the Light to Come:** *In turn, prophets (P) process with a lit candle, placing it on a stand before they present their text. The portion of the passage that relates to light is shown below.*

*P1:* Isaiah 42:6–7 *"You will be a light to guide the nations . . ."*

*P2:* Jeremiah 31:35–40 *"It is the LORD who provides the sun to light the day . . ."*

*P3:* Micah 7:8–10 *"The LORD will be my light . . ."*

*P4:* Habakkuk 3:3–4, 6 *"His coming is as brilliant as the sunrise . . ."*]

*P5:* Zechariah 14:6–7, 9 *"On that day . . . there will be continuous day . . ."*

*P6:* Malachi 4:2–4 *"The Sun of Righteousness will rise . . ."*

*P7:* Luke 2:29–32 *"He is a light to reveal God to the nations . . ."*

[Congregational song proclaiming or responding to Christ as the light]

**Juxtaposition I: The Light Is Arrested**

*Cross:* John 18:1b–11 *"Jesus crossed the Kidron Valley with his disciples . . ."*

*One of the seven candles is extinguished.*

*Light:* John 12:35–36a, 44–46, 49–50 *"My light will shine for you just a little longer . . ."*

[Optional congregational response]

**Juxtaposition II: The Light Is Questioned**

*Cross:* John 18:12–14, 19–24 *"So the soldiers . . . arrested Jesus . . ."*

*One of the six remaining candles is extinguished.*

*Light:* John 11:1, 3–11 *"Our friend Lazarus has fallen asleep, but now I will go and wake him up."*

[Optional congregational response]

**Juxtaposition III: The Light Is Denied**

*Cross:* John 18:15–18, 25–27 *"Simon Peter followed Jesus . . ."*

*One of the five remaining candles is extinguished.*

*Light:* John 9:1–7, 35–41 *" . . . Go wash yourself in the pool of Siloam . . ."*

[Optional congregational response]

**Juxtaposition IV: The Light Is Accused**

*Cross:* John 18:28–40 *"Jesus' trial before Caiaphas ended . . ."*

*One of the four remaining candles is extinguished.*

*Light:* John 8:1–12 *"Where are your accusers? . . ."*
[Optional congregational response]

**Juxtaposition V: The Light Is Mocked**
*Cross:* John 19:1–16 *"Then Pilate had Jesus flogged . . ."*
*One of the three remaining candles is extinguished.*

*Light:* John 3:17–21 *"God's light came into the world . . ."*
[Optional congregational response]

**Juxtaposition VI: The Light Is Crucified**
*Cross:* John 19:16–27 *"Pilate turned Jesus over to them to be crucified . . ."*
*One of the two remaining candles is extinguished.*

*Light:* John 1:1–5 *"The light shines in the darkness . . ."*
[Optional congregational response]

**Juxtaposition VII: The Light Dies**
*Cross:* John 19:28–30 *"Jesus knew that his mission was now finished . . ."*

*The final candle is extinguished. The service is over. Allow people to stay as long as they'd like in silence.*

## GOOD FRIDAY: TESTIMONIES

In an attempt to embrace the humanness of Christ's act on the cross, this Good Friday service of testimonies focuses on Christ's willingness to lay down his life and on what exactly he was giving up. This service starts similar to a funeral and is unique in telling the narrative of Christ's death at the *beginning* of the service by Matthew,

Mark, Luke, and John (preferably memorized). The remainder of the service is spent on everything that happened between Christ's death and his resurrection. In the little information provided about this time period, we get a fuller understanding of everything Christ was sacrificing on the cross. His submission is then expounded upon through testimonies from your own congregation. In hearing members of your congregation identify with Christ as he surrendered his work, gave up proving something, let go of someone who did not yet understand, left people he cared deeply about, surrendered his body, and gave up his control, we might more fully recognize the wonder of Christ's humanity and his love for all of creation. See the basic service structure below.

**The Crucifixion:** *From Matthew 27:35–50; Mark 15:24–37; Luke 23:32–46; and John 19:18–30.*

*The Christ candle is processed in (already lit).*

| | |
|---|---|
| *Matthew:* | The crucifixion of our Lord according to the Gospel of Matthew, |
| *Mark:* | the Gospel of Mark, |
| *Luke:* | the Gospel of Luke, |
| *John:* | and the Gospel of John. |
| *Matthew:* | After they had nailed him to the cross, the soldiers gambled for his clothes by throwing dice. |
| *John:* | They divided his clothes among the four of them. They also took his robe, but it was seamless, woven in one piece from top to bottom. So they said, "Rather than tearing it apart, let's throw dice for it." This fulfilled the Scripture that says, "They divided my garments among themselves and threw dice for my clothing." |
| *Matthew:* | Then they sat around and kept guard as he hung there. |

*John:* Pilate posted a sign on the cross.

*Matthew:* It read, "This is Jesus,

*Mark:* the King of the Jews."

*John:* The place where Jesus was crucified was near the city, and the sign was written in Hebrew, Latin, and Greek, so that many people could read it. Then the leading priests objected and said to Pilate, "Change it from 'The King of the Jews' to 'He said, I am King of the Jews.'" Pilate replied, "No, what I have written, I have written."

*Luke:* Two others, both criminals, were led out to be executed with him.

*Mark:* Two revolutionaries,

*Matthew:* one on his right and one on his left.

*Luke:* One of the criminals hanging beside him scoffed, "So you're the Messiah, are you? Prove it by saving yourself—and us, too, while you're at it!" But the other criminal protested, "Don't you fear God even when you have been sentenced to die? We deserve to die for our crimes, but this man hasn't done anything wrong." Then he said, "Jesus, remember me when you come into your Kingdom." And Jesus replied, "I assure you, today you will be with me in paradise."

*Mark:* The people passing by shouted abuse, shaking their heads in mockery. "Ha! Look at you now!" they yelled at him. "You said you were going to destroy the Temple and rebuild it in three days. Well then, save yourself and come down from the cross!"

*Matthew:* The leading priests, the teachers of religious law, and the elders also mocked Jesus.

*Luke:* "He saved others," they said, "let him save himself if he is really God's Messiah, the Chosen One."

*John:* Standing near the cross were Jesus' mother, and his mother's sister, Mary, and Mary Magdalene. When Jesus saw his mother standing there beside the disciple he loved, he said to her, "Dear woman, here is your son." And he said to this disciple, "Here is your mother." And from then on this disciple took her into his home.

*Mark:* It was nine o'clock in the morning when they crucified him.

*Luke:* At noon, darkness fell across the whole land until three o'clock.

*Mark:* Then at three Jesus called out with a loud voice, "*Eloi, Eloi, lema sabachthani?*"

*Matthew:* Which means, "My God, my God, why have you abandoned me?"

*Mark:* Some of the bystanders misunderstood and thought he was calling the prophet Elijah.

*John:* Jesus knew that his mission was now finished, and to fulfill Scripture he said, "I am thirsty." A jar of sour wine was sitting there, so they soaked a sponge in it, put it on a hyssop branch, and held it up to his lips.

*Matthew:* But the rest said, "Wait! Let's see whether Elijah comes to save him."

*Mark:* Then Jesus uttered another loud cry.

*Matthew:* He shouted,

*Luke:* "Father, I entrust my spirit into your hands!"

*John:* "It is finished!"

*Luke:* And with those words,

*John:* he bowed his head

*Luke and Mark:* and breathed his last

*Matthew & John:* and he released his Spirit.

*Christ candle is extinguished.*

[Congregational song in response to the death of Christ]

**Testimony I:**

*Luke:* Luke 23:45 *"The light from the sun was gone . . ."*

*Testimony 1:* Even in his death, Christ was in control. He chose not to stay and answer all the questions his ministry had provoked, but instead chose to surrender his work to the Father's plan.

*Testimony identifying with Christ's surrendering of his work.*

[Optional congregational response]

**Testimony II:**

*John:* John 19:31–37 *"It was the day of preparation . . ."*

*Testimony 2:* Even in his death, Christ was in control. He chose not to prove anything about himself, but instead chose to lay down his life in perfect fulfillment of his Word.

*Testimony identifying with Christ's giving up proving something.*

[Optional congregational response]

**Testimony III:**

*Luke:* Luke 23:47 *"When the Roman officer . . . saw what had happened . . ."*

*Testimony 3:* Even in his death, Christ was in control. He did not get to witness the worship of the centurion but chose death without the promise that anyone would change their mind about him.

*Testimony identifying with Christ's letting go of his sheep.*

[Optional congregational response]

**Testimony IV:**

*Luke:* Luke 23:49 *"But Jesus' friends . . . stood at a distance watching."*

*Testimony 4:* Even in his death, Christ was in control. He chose not to remain with those he loved but chose to leave them in the care of others.

*Testimony identifying with Christ's giving up of relationships.*
**[Optional congregational response]**

**Testimony V:**

| | |
|---|---|
| *Mark:* | Mark 15:43–47 *"Joseph . . . took Jesus' body down from the cross, wrapped it in the cloth, and laid it in a tomb . . . ."* |
| *Testimony 5:* | Even in his death, Christ was in control. He chose not to run from the bitter cup of physical death, but chose to die, facing mortality, and surrendering his body into the care of others. |

*Testimony identifying with Christ's mortality.*
**[Optional congregational response]**

**Testimony VI:**

| | |
|---|---|
| *Matthew:* | Matthew 27:62–66 *"The next day, on the Sabbath . . ."* |
| *Testimony 6:* | Even in his death, Christ was in control when he chose not to take control. Instead, he chose to submit that control to those he left behind. |

*Testimony identifying with Christ's surrendering of control.*
**[Optional congregational response]**

Christ candle is processed out of the dark sanctuary. Consider using an audio track of the closing of a tomb. Allow people to stay as long as they'd like in silence.

## GOOD FRIDAY: FLASHBACKS

The following offers the most theatrical option of all the services in this resource. The service is comprised of six flashbacks from characters watching Jesus approach the cross. Each flashback gets progressively further from the cross while the narrative itself journeys forward with Christ to the cross. The last flashback is Mary remembering Christ's birth while the narrative is of her watching him die. These scripted flashbacks are obviously fiction, but the characters and much of the content was transposed from the biblical texts. The congregation might even hear their own questions in many of these characters' stories as we wrestle with the mysteries of Christ's work on the cross.

You might discover a way to create a simple set for each character to present their flashback within. A basin of water for John; a jar of perfume for Mary the sister of Lazarus; a fishing net for Peter; five loaves of bread and two fish for the boy; a decorative pillar for Simeon; and a manger for Mary, the mother of Jesus. As with the service of contrast, you'll notice that this service also offers the option to incorporate the tradition of Tenebrae, successively extinguishing candles as each scene plays out.

**Scene I:**

*Narrator:* Mark 14:32–41 *The Garden of Gethsemane*

*John:* *John remembers Jesus washing the disciples' feet (see John 13:1–17)*

It had been another long day together, and the time of Passover had come. It was around supper time that night, and the rest of the disciples and I were ready to eat. We eagerly sat down together, when suddenly, deliberately, Jesus got up from the table.

We watched him, resolute and calm as he was, take off his outer robe, wrap a towel around his waist, pick up a jar of water, and fill a basin with it. His movement from the table to the floor quickly silenced the room. What was he doing?

He knelt in front of me, stretched out his arm, and took my foot in his hand. He began to wash my feet, first my right, then my left. They were filthy with the dust of a day's journey—cracked by the many miles we had traveled together. I was confused. Stunned. Moved. Horrified.

And as he washed my feet, he looked up and our eyes met. Part of me wanted to look away, almost embarrassed that I was letting this man I respect so much serve me in such a way; yet, I could not look away. His love captivated me.

After he finished drying each foot with the towel that was wrapped around him, he moved to the disciple next to me, knelt down, and began to wash his feet; then he moved to the next, and to the next. Some put up a fight, but soon all had submitted themselves to accepting this act of service.

I have never known friendship like this. Up to this point, Jesus had been my leader, my mentor, my idol—the person I wanted to be like yet always felt was on a higher level. And now, I watched him stoop so low to serve us. How *much* did this man love us? Why were we cherished so deeply? Was it possible for him to stoop any lower for the ones he loved?

I had never been loved like this, and yet it wasn't but a couple hours later that my friend, my brother, needed me and I failed him. "Keep watch and pray," he told us. I should have known something was coming; I should have sensed the looming threat. Why was I not a better friend to him like he was to me? Why couldn't I stay awake? Why did I choose to sleep instead of praying with him?[6]

*Extinguish first candle.*

[Optional congregational response]

**Scene II:**

*Narrator:* Matthew 26:47–51, 55–56 *Judas Betrays Jesus*

*Mary (sister): Mary, the sister of Lazarus, anoints Jesus (see John 12:3)*

It was six days ago. Jesus came to my brother Lazarus' house for dinner. The last time Jesus had visited us, it had been under darker circumstances. Lazarus had just died, and we thought Jesus had only come to pay his respects; but, to everyone's disbelief, Jesus had the stone rolled away from the tomb and called Lazarus from death back to life. Saying it now, I still have to remind myself that it all actually happened—that it wasn't a dream. Jesus gave us back our brother! He turned my wailing into dancing; he removed my sorrow and clothed me with joy. How could my heart be still? How could I not praise my Lord forever?!

So, as Martha began to serve Jesus and his disciples along with Lazarus, I snuck away to grab a jar of perfume that I had been saving; it had taken me an entire year to save enough money to finally buy it. There was no gift adequate to show the true depth of my appreciation for Jesus or one that would be worthy of who he was, but I had to do something. He was different, set apart—he was holy—and we all knew he had a sacred purpose, even if we didn't know exactly what it was.

I took the perfume and made my way to the table where Jesus was. I shouldn't have gone to the table; I wasn't permitted. But in light of who Jesus was, even cultural standards seemed to fade away. I wanted to be near him. I wanted to love him as he had loved my family.

I poured the perfume all over his feet, and I used my hair to spread it around. The room went silent as the fragrance filled the house. The moment was heavy and still. But the stillness was upset by Judas' condemning voice. "That money should have been given to the poor!" he yelled. I paused, turning my head to see his face. He was angry, livid even. Mad at my adoration. His rage was unfounded, corrupt, blinded by his own thievery.

Why didn't he understand? Did he not realize that the last time I was at Jesus' feet I was weeping over my brother's death—the very brother that now sat fully alive across from him? Did he not understand who Jesus was? What he could do? What he *was* doing?

He didn't understand it then, and he doesn't understand it now. Judas saw miracles, he saw people changed, brought back to life—how could he be so close to Jesus and not be changed by him? Why did he fear love so much?

I consecrated Christ with oil; Judas betrayed him with a kiss. Oh, how the sweet fragrance has changed to a bitter stench; a dark odor that spreads deep within.

*Extinguish second candle.*

[Optional congregational response]

**Scene III:**

*Narrator:* Mark 14:66–72 *Peter's Denial*

*Peter:* *Peter walks on water (see Matt. 14:22–33)*

We were headed across the lake—the other disciples and I—the sun had just set when the winds began to pick up. Jesus had stayed behind, because he wanted some time alone to think and pray, but his absence made the approaching storm feel all the more ominous. Hours passed, but the storm didn't. The waves grew higher, the wind stronger, and we were helpless to fight them—we could only let them take us where they wanted, while we tried to stay afloat.

The crashing of the waves and the roar of the wind made it almost impossible to hear the frantic cries of the other disciples as we tried to keep the boat afloat, but our ears instantly sharpened when one of the disciples cried out, "It's a ghost!"

And indeed, there was someone—a man walking across the water toward us, as though it was solid ground. Before any of us could react or say anything, the figure shouted, "Don't be afraid! I'm here!" No one said it—no one said anything—but we all knew it was Jesus. But, were we dreaming? How was this possible? He was walking securely on water in the middle of a violent storm!

I yelled back to him, "If it's really you, then let me walk on the water to you!" And so he yelled back, "Come out of the boat, Peter!"

After I said it, I wasn't sure if I really wanted to do what I had just asked, but it was a moment in which my body was responding faster than my mind. I clutched the side of the boat, looked at the waves, but then looked up and saw my friend staring back with such peace amidst such storm. His peace gave me the confidence I needed. I leapt out of the boat and I didn't sink; I stood for a second and I saw Jesus smile slightly. I began to walk toward him, my eyes never leaving his as I wanted nothing more than to be near him.

I had forgotten about the storm around me until a wave crashed into me. At that moment, I realized the weight of the wind from every direction. I looked down, recognizing for the first time that my feet were firmly on water! My mind began to catch up. Adrenalin surged through my body; my heart raced, my legs shook. I went to my knees thinking I'd catch myself as I began to fall, but I couldn't stay above the storm. I was in it now—fully submerged—being tossed about in the waves; I threw my hands in the air reaching for someone to save me.

Jesus quickly came to me and pulled me up. I clung to him as my safety, and my first instinct was to think, "Why did you let that happen? Didn't you see that I was afraid?" But Jesus simply asked, "Why did you doubt me?"

Why *did* I doubt him? Why was I so afraid? I had seen him do so many miraculous things for *other* people; why was it so difficult for *me* to trust him?

Three times, he said, I'd deny him; three separate times I'd lie about the past three years of being with him. I walked on water with this man—never did I think I'd be capable of denying knowing him. He changed my life; he was my best friend; he was my mentor; he was my Lord . . . But once again, I looked down at my own feet; I looked at the storm around me and I was afraid.

*Extinguish third candle.*

[Optional congregational response]

**Scene IV:**

*Narrator:* Luke 23:13–25 *Jesus with Pilate before the Crowd*

*Boy:* *A boy offers his lunch and Jesus feeds thousands (see John 6:1–14)*

I had been standing all day. And for the most part I couldn't even hear what the man was saying. A kid my age doesn't exactly get front row seats to hear Jesus talk. My body was tired from straining to hear and see, and so I decided to sit down, away from the crowd. But as soon as I had pulled out my lunch, I saw a man waving frantically at me. "You! Boy! What's that you're eating?" he yelled.

I stared up at him, and timidly showed the five loaves of bread and two fish my mother had packed. The man crouched down and got close to my face. "We need this food to feed this crowd."

The look I gave him must have shown my disbelief—there were after all, thousands of people here. But somehow, I was nodding yes, and the next thing I knew, he had grabbed my arm and began moving his way quickly through the people. The longer we moved the faster he began to walk, until we were almost sprinting up the crest of the hill. And then suddenly, there he was: Jesus, the man I had been trying to see all day, staring straight at me.

The disciple told him that I had food. "But what good is that going to do?" they asked him. Jesus didn't respond. He simply walked over to me, put his hand on my shoulder, and smiled. "Go tell the people to sit down," he said to his disciples. He took the food from my hands, and with the most trusting eyes I've ever seen, looked up into the heavens and began to pray.

What happened next was nothing short of a miracle. He began to break the bread . . . and break the bread . . .

and kept breaking the bread. It never stopped! Same with the fish! I must have rubbed my eyes a hundred times! But every time I looked, there was more food.

The people were starting to get excited. I could hear them clearly now. They were energized by the food and some were even starting to beg for Jesus to be their king. I looked back to see what Jesus would do next, only . . . he was gone.

But now, standing in Pilate's courtyard with yet another crowd, I saw him again. This time though, they weren't yelling for him to be their king. They were yelling for him to be crucified. I couldn't stop the tears from rolling down my face, or the anger burning in my throat.

What changed? What happened? How could they love him in one moment and hate him in another? Had they forgotten so quickly? Why could the One who satisfied so many with so little now only satisfy them by giving so much?

*Extinguish fourth candle.*

[Optional congregational response]

**Scene V:**

*Narrator:* John 19:1–6 *Jesus Is Mocked*

*Simeon:* *Simeon holds Jesus in his arms (see Luke 2:25–35)*

I remember holding him in my arms: the manifestation of the hope of salvation for Israel. Years upon years, I had waited for this sign, and now God's promise to the world was gently laid in my outstretched arms. I saw with my own eyes and felt with my own hands the love and faithfulness of my Lord displayed in a small vulnerable baby. Centuries of incessant and seemingly fruitless anticipation dissolved in one sweet moment orchestrated by the Spirit of God. The moment still stands at the forefront of my mind and always will.

As I laid my hand on his small head and looked to the heavens, I said, "I have seen your salvation, which you have prepared for all people. He is a light to reveal God to the nations, and he is the glory of your people Israel!" But as I then boldly declared, "Lord, now let your servant depart in peace," I now faintly echo those words as I beg for God to vindicate his salvation from being destroyed by the very world he came to save.

Where is salvation now? Where is the light, promised to be revealed? Where is your glory as your Son takes hit, after hit, after hit of the reed? A twisted and contorted crown of thorns digs into his skull as the boy I once exalted receives blow after blow and is stung with the disrespect of men's spit and cutting curses. Oh, to hold him now.

Did he really leave his transcendence for this? How could the baby that was held so high, now be brought so low? How could this lead to salvation? How could this be God's plan for the world?

How long, oh Jehovah? How long will you hide your face from this world? Will you not show us your salvation? Will you not have pity on your servant and most beloved?

I knew he would be opposed, I said it to his mother; but like this? I proclaimed that the deepest thoughts of many hearts would be revealed by him, but *dark* are the hearts that are being revealed on this God-forsaken day.

Lord, could you bring glory from this man even now?

*Extinguish fifth candle.*
[Optional congregational response]

**Scene VI:**

*Narrator:* John 19:16b–26 *Jesus on the Cross*

*Mary (mother): Mary the Mother of Jesus (see Luke 1:26–38, 46–56; 2:1–7, 16–19)*

In the beginning, I wondered if it would be the longest nine months of my life. The gossiping whispers, the stares, my family's silence. . . . In those first weeks, it seemed more than I would be able to bear. In the most acute moments of isolation and questioning, I clung to the words of the messenger God had sent me, sometimes saying them out loud to remind myself for reassurance: "Don't be afraid, Mary . . . He will be called the Son of the Most High . . . His kingdom will never end."

As we made the journey to Bethlehem; as nearly every person we asked for help turned us away; as I, just a girl myself, lay in the straw and hay of a stable, discovering for the first time the piercing pains of childbirth—there were any number of reasons for me to question if God really knew what he was doing. Yet, he proved himself faithful again and again.

When my son arrived—the One I had been promised, that *my people* had been promised for centuries, the Messiah—I held him in my arms . . . so small, so helpless, and frail. I was reminded that the Holy One does great things. Holy is his name.

Now, those nine months of uncertainty, the public ridicule, the labor . . . it all seems like a flash of time in comparison to the hours I've spent here watching my little boy, Jesus, Immanuel, suffer. I hear every insult the crowd speaks to him, I see every offensive gesture, every act of aggression . . . I have no more tears; my spirit is downcast within me. My nausea is the only proof that my body can still feel; my pulse taunts me as it reminds me beat after beat that I cannot escape this reality.

How can the God who would take such care in bringing his Son to earth—in protecting him from the vile acts of Herod, in providing for him as he healed the sick and proclaimed the Word to the masses—now allow him such suffering and grief? What hope could come from this? What is salvation, if this is the cost?

(To the Father)

Am I still favored by you, O God? Why then must I face such agony? You said you would give him the throne of David—that his kingdom would never end! What kind of throne is a cross?! What kind of kingdom comes from death? How can this be?

I am the Lord's servant. May everything you have said come true . . . everything.

(To her Son)

Do not be afraid my child, Son of the Most High . . . your kingdom will never end.

*Extinguish sixth candle.*

[Optional congregational response]

**Scene VII:**

*Narrator:* Mark 15:33–39 *Christ dies*

*The seventh candle, still lit, is processed out of the sanctuary, hidden from our eyes until Easter morning. The service is over. Allow people to stay as long as they'd like in silence.*

## ORDINARY TIME SPECIAL SERVICE: THE CHRISTIAN YEAR

Below is a journey through the entirety of the Christian Year in one service. You could offer this as an evening service anytime during Ordinary Time, offering a reminder, preparation, or even a teaching on the Christian Year, while being in the longest season. However, it seems most appropriate to celebrate this service on Christ the King Sunday, either as a special service or in place of the regular morning worship service. Used on this day, the Christian Year service acts as a concluding celebration of the Christian year. We remember—in one service—the full story of Christ before beginning, once again, the season of Advent the following week.

If you celebrate the Christian calendar throughout the year, this service shouldn't require much additional work, as it basically invites you to compile all the elements you've facilitated throughout the previous year's seasons. In fact, to better allow your people to engage with this service, it would be wise to pull from elements already included in your annual liturgy versus copying and pasting the service order provided here. However, hopefully, this sample can inspire ways of organizing your current practices, so that your congregation is able to fully engage as, together, you journey through the life of Christ.

### Advent:

*Altar cloth is changed to blue/purple.*

[Congregational Advent song with prophecies (P) declared between stanzas]

*P1:* Isaiah 64:1–4 (*first blue/purple candle is lit/placed*)
*P2:* Isaiah 64:5–6a, 8–9 (*second blue/purple candle is lit/placed*)
*P3:* Isaiah 61:1–2a (*pink candle is lit/placed*)
*P4:* Isaiah 40:1–5 (*third blue/purple candle is lit/placed*)
*P5:* Isaiah 9:6 (*Christ candle is lit/placed*)

### Christmas:

*Altar cloth is changed to white.*

[Congregational Christmas song: *Consider the inclusion of a living nativity scene, perhaps even built in correlation with a verse of the song.*]

### Epiphany:

*Altar cloth is changed to green.*

[Congregational song about Christ's presence and work on earth (excluding the cross or the resurrection)]

[Giving of Tithes & Offerings: *Consider connecting your giving to the gifts of the magi.*]

[Scripture Presentation: *Consider creating "Kids' Scripture Videos" to present these stories.*]

Matthew 2:1–2, 9c–11 *The magi visit Jesus*
Mark 1:9–13 *Jesus' baptism*
John 2:1–11 *Jesus turns water into wine*

[Scripture Presentation: *Consider presenting this text with tableau scenes.*]

Mark 9:2–10 *The transfiguration*

**Lent:**

*Altar cloth is changed to purple.*

[Congregational song asking God for mercy: *Presider is imposed with ashes*]

[Prayer of Confession: *Led by Presider*]

[Assurance of Pardon: *Led by Presider*]

[Congregational song praising God for his mercy]

*Altar cloth is changed to red for Holy Week.*

[Presentation of Scripture: *Consider using a musical underscore with the presentation of these texts. Have a character for each reading present the text, preferably from memory, as though they were witnesses to the scene.*]

John 12:12–19 *The triumphal entry*

*Altar cloth is changed to black for Good Friday.*

John 18:1–8, 12 *The grove of olive trees*

John 19:17–18a, 28–30 *Jesus dies*

*Silence (and possibly darkness).*

**Easter:** *Consider how you might allow the congregation to experience this dramatic shift in ethos. Should it be quick with bursting light or restrained with a slow crescendo of sound?*

*Altar cloth is changed to white.*

[Congregational Easter song 1]

[Easter Greeting]

*Leader:* He is risen!

***All:*** He is risen indeed!

[Congregational Greeting/Passing of the Peace]

[Congregational Easter song 2]

*Altar cloth is changed to red for Pentecost.*

[Scripture Presentation]

Acts 2:1–8, 11–12, 40–41 *Pentecost*

[Congregational song praising the Holy Spirit]

**Ordinary Time:**

*Altar cloth is changed to green.*

[The Apostles' Creed]

[Prayers of the People: *Led by Presider*]

[Eucharistic Prayer: *(1) Thank God for his work of salvation epitomized in Christ. (2) Remember Christ's words when he took bread, blessed it, broke it, and gave it (see Matt. 26:26–28; Mark 14:22–24; Luke 22:19–20 or 24:30; John 6:11). (3) Ask the Holy Spirit to bless the elements.*]

[Invitation to the Table]

[Communion]

[Benediction: *Give a scriptural blessing to the congregation as you send them out to reveal Christ's life to the world.*]

# EPILOGUE

Tell the story of Christ! May this be the primary objective you take away from this resource. Amidst all the seasons, all the planning, all the special Sundays, the special services, the colors, and the creativity, never lose sight of Christ. The Christian Year is not the objective. Your church's understanding and adherence to the Christian Year is not the objective. *Christ is the objective!* My offering of this resource comes only from my experience and deep appreciation of the Christian Year as a primary tool to knowing Christ more. It also acts as a method to holding our context accountable to telling the full story of Christ, not just the parts we like. And there is a mystical and ecclesiological beauty in adhering to this annual means of telling Christ's life as it began to be developed as early as the second century.

Every church has a set of primary values—maybe it's good preaching, the use of the arts, congregational care, hospitality, theological knowledge, good music, community involvement, and the list goes on and on. These are all good things to excel in, but they are secondary. Christ—and his narrative proclaimed in Scripture—should be our highest goal. It is your job every week to help your people see Christ and invite them to lives of response. It is in telling Christ's story that we see narrative enact theology, sermons bring Christ to our context, care and hospitality reveal divine nature, the arts point to wonders beyond themselves, and community involvement grows as a natural response. Never lose sight of the living, breathing Christ, for our work is lifeless and void when he is not at the center.

As I mentioned at the start of this resource, everything we do is forming us into someone. The question is less about what you want to do and more about who you are becoming (because of what you're *already* doing). In remembering Christ and his story, we are being formed into the likeness of our Creator, the one who knows us best and loves us best. We center our lives around his story so that we might be formed into his likeness and take part in his kingdom-coming work. I invite you, therefore, to tell the story of Christ. Live his life in your contexts as a corporate body. Make him the center of your worship, and watch as his life transforms the life of your church.

# NOTES

## INTRODUCTION: WHY A BOOK ABOUT THE CHRISTIAN YEAR?

1. The lectionary is a compilation of assigned Scripture readings for a particular day. Readings from the Old Testament, Psalms, Epistles, and Gospels are organized thematically (correlating with the Christian Year) over a three-year cycle (Years A, B, and C). These texts are included in this resource, not as required texts, but as a historic resource that can be beneficial in inspiring and developing ideas, as well as giving your creativity focus.

As a point of indication: Years that are divisible by 3 will start Year A in Advent. For example, because 2019 is divisible by 3, Year A begins in Advent of 2019 and continues into the following seasons of 2020.

Parenthesis used in the assigned psalm indicate a shorter selection of verses that could be read in place of the entire psalm. Parenthesis used in all other references indicate optional additional verses that could be included with the assigned readings.

2. Thomas Howard, *Evangelical Is Not Enough: Worship of God in Liturgy and Sacrament* (San Francisco, CA: Ignatius Press, 1984), 131–32.

3. In this understanding of worship, I have been deeply impacted by the writings of Robert Webber and Constance Cherry. For more in-depth resources on revelation and response and the dialogical nature of worship see:

Robert E. Webber, *Worship Is a Verb: Celebrating God's Mighty Deeds of Salvation* (Peabody, MA: Hendrickson Publishers, 2004), and Constance M. Cherry, "Establishing the Foundation: Biblical Worship," in *The Worship Architect: A Blueprint for Designing Culturally Relevant and Biblically Faithful Services* (Grand Rapids, MI: Baker Academic, 2010) 3–18.

4. Antoine de Saint-Exupéry, *The Wisdom of the Sands* (New York: Harcourt Brace, 1950), quoted in James K. A. Smith, *You Are What You Love: The Spiritual Power of Habit* (Grand Rapids, MI: Brazos Press, 2016), 11.

## MOVEMENT I—ADVENT: THE INVITATION TO ANTICIPATE CHRIST'S COMING

1. See Athanasius, *On the Incarnation of the Word*, 54:3.

## MOVEMENT II—CHRISTMAS: THE INVITATION TO CELEBRATE CHRIST'S PRESENCE ON EARTH

1. I say "would have" simply because these dates are the days the church has chosen to remember this portion of the story. They are not the actual dates of the original events. For more information on the origins of the seasons that make up the Christian Year as well as the history of how they came to have their assigned length of time and place in the calendar, see Paul Bradshaw and Maxwell Johnson, *The Origins of Feasts, Fasts, and Seasons in Early Christianity* (London, Great Britain: Society for Promoting Christian Knowledge; Collegeville, MN: Liturgical Press, 2011).

2. Author unknown (oldest known: Robert Croo), "Coventry Carol" (sixteenth century), public domain.

3. Author unknown, "The First Noel the Angel Did Say" (1833), public domain.

## MOVEMENT III—EPIPHANY: THE INVITATION TO WONDER AT CHRIST'S WORK ON EARTH

1. Compilation of Epiphany stories presented by kids from College Wesleyan Church (Marion, IN, 2017): https://www.youtube.com/watch?v=N9S1jYXebVM.

2. David L. Stubbs, "Ethics" in *A More Profound Alleluia*, ed. Leanne Van Dyk (Grand Rapids, MI: Wm. B. Eerdmans Publishing Co., 2005), 136.

## MOVEMENT IV—LENT: THE INVITATION TO RECKON OUR LIFE WITH CHRIST'S LIFE AND DEATH

1. It is common to hear that the season of Lent is forty days. When considering the season as a period of fasting, this statement is still true. One does not fast on Sundays. Even though the season of Lent is forty-six days in actuality, the Lenten fast is only forty days because it does not include the six Sundays within the season.

2. James K. A. Smith, *You Are What You Love: The Spiritual Power of Habit* (Grand Rapids, MI: Brazos Press, 2016), 97.

3. See *The Worship Sourcebook* (Grand Rapids, MI: Calvin Institute of Christian Worship; Faith Alive Christian Resources; and Baker Books, 2013).

4. "Transposing Scripture" was coined by F. Russell Mitmann in *Worship in the Shape of Scripture* (Cleveland, OH: The Pilgrim Press, 2001).

5. *The Book of Common Prayer* (New York: Oxford University Press, 2007), 352.

6. James K. A. Smith, *You Are What You Love: The Spiritual Power of Habit* (Grand Rapids, MI: Brazos Press, 2016), 104.

## MOVEMENT V—EASTER: THE INVITATION TO TRIUMPH WITH CHRIST OVER SIN AND DEATH

1. Athanasius, *On the Incarnation of the Word*, 4.20.

2. Athanasius, *On the Incarnation of the Word*, 25.3. "Become a curse" refers to Galatians 3:13.

3. See Gustaf Aulén on the Greek Fathers' views of God's righteousness within the Atonement. Gustaf Aulén, *Christus Victor: An Historical Study of the Three Main Types of the Idea of the Atonement* (New York: Macmillan Publishing Co., Inc., 1969), 44–45.

4. Athanasius, *On the Incarnation of the Word*, 27.3.

5. "Easter" as a verb taken from Gerard Manley Hopkins' poem "The Wreck of the Deutschland."

6. See Steve DeNeff, *More Than Forgiveness: Following Jesus into the Heart of Holiness* (Indianapolis, IN: Wesleyan Publishing House, 2011), 60.

7. Jeff Barker, Professor of Theatre and Speech, offers many creative ideas and methods for sharing testimonies in his book *The Storytelling Church: Adventures in Reclaiming the Role of Story in Worship* (Cleveland, TN: Webber Institute Books, 2011).

8. Augustine, *Questions on the Heptateuch,* III, 84 (c. 410) and *Against Faustus the Manichaean,* XIX, 11 (c. 398), translated by Bernard Leeming, in James F. White, *Documents of Christian Worship: Descriptive and Interpretive Sources* (Louisville, KY: Westminster John Knox Press, 1992), 120.

9. For more on sacramental theology, see James F. White, "God's Love Made Visible" in *Introduction to Christian Worship* (Nashville, TN: Abingdon Press, 2000), 175–201.

10. Constance Cherry, *The Worship Architect: A Blueprint for Designing Culturally Relevant and Biblically Faithful Services* (Grand Rapids, MI: Baker Academic, 2010), 217.

11. "The eighth day" specifically refers to the culmination of the Festival of Shelters in Leviticus 23:33–43. Though a normal week is seven days, God calls both the first and the eighth days holy and days of rest in this festival. The eighth day, though it is just the first day of the following week, is both the end of the previous week *and* the start of the next week. In comparing Holy Week with the seven days of creation laid out in Genesis, one can't help but gain a new perspective in seeing God rest again—though, this time in a tomb—on the seventh day. But unlike the first genesis, the Easter narrative includes an eighth day on which Holy Week culminates with an ending on the day after the seventh day that was also a new beginning for the whole world. Therefore, believers meet on the eighth day: the end and the beginning. The previous week ends in the gathering of the believers and another week begins in the sending of the believers. The eighth day applies to Pentecost too (even if just allegorically) as it is the ending or culmination of the Easter season, and yet it is the beginning of the church.

12. Robert E. Webber, *The Divine Embrace: Recovering the Passionate Spiritual Life* (Grand Rapids, MI: Baker Books, 2006), 149.

13. For a greater exposition on the connection between Babel and Pentecost, see Timothy M. Pierce, *Enthroned on Our Praise: An Old Testament Theology of Worship* (Nashville, TN: B & H Publishing Group, 2008), 39–40.

## MOVEMENT VI—ORDINARY TIME: THE INVITATION TO COMMIT TO CHRIST THROUGH THE CHURCH

1. Constance Cherry, *The Worship Architect: A Blueprint for Designing Culturally Relevant and Biblically Faithful Services* (Grand Rapids, MI: Baker Academic, 2010), 215.
2. For a reverse lectionary database, see www.textweek.com/scripture.htm.

## TELLING CHRIST'S STORY BEYOND THE SUNDAY GATHERING

1. Constance Cherry, *The Worship Architect: A Blueprint for Designing Culturally Relevant and Biblically Faithful Services* (Grand Rapids, MI.: Baker Academic, 2010), 210.
2. See "Discipleship Ministries: The United Methodist Church" at https://www.umcdiscipleship.org.
3. "O Come, O Come, Emmanuel" (1861 translation of "Veni, veni, Emmanuel"), lyrics translated by John Mason Neale (1818–1866), music by Thomas Helmore (1811–1890), public domain.
4. When retelling common biblical narratives, consider using *THE MESSAGE* by Eugene H. Peterson, or *The Jesus Storybook Bible: Every Story Whispers His Name*, written by Sally Lloyd-Jones and illustrated by Jago.
5. *The Book of Common Prayer* (New York: Oxford University Press, 2007), 217.
6. This Good Friday "Flashbacks" script was written by members of College Wesleyan Church, Marion, Indiana (2015): Scene I (John): Liz Simmons; Scene II (Mary, sister of Lazarus): Judy Crossman; Scene III (Peter): Daniel Rife; Scene IV (Boy): Jordan Rife; Scene V (Simeon): Alan Murphy; Scene VI (Mary, mother of Jesus): Emily Vermilya. Edited by Daniel Rife.

# FOR FURTHER STUDY


Cherry, Constance M. "Encountering God in the Christian Year: Remembering the Whole Narrative." In *The Worship Architect: A Blueprint for Designing Culturally Relevant and Biblically Faithful Services*, 205–218. Grand Rapids, MI: Baker Academic, 2010.

Floyd, Pat. *The Special Days and Seasons of the Christian Year: How They Came About and How They Are Observed by Christians Today*. Nashville, TN: Abingdon Press, 1998.

Gross, Bobby. *Living the Christian Year: Time to Inhabit the Story of God*. Downers Grove, IL: Intervarsity Press, 2009.

Hickman, Hoyt L., Don E. Saliers, Laurence Hull Stookey, and James F. White. *Handbook of the Christian Year*. Nashville, TN: Abingdon Press, 1986.

Howard, Thomas. "The Liturgical Year: Redeeming the Time." In *Evangelical Is Not Enough: Worship of God in Liturgy and Sacrament*, 131–148. San Francisco, CA: Ignatius Press, 1984.

Pfatteicher, Philip H. *Journey into the Heart of God: Living the Liturgical Year*. New York: Oxford University Press, 2013.

Stookey, Laurence Hull. *Calendar: Christ's Time for the Church*. Nashville, TN: Abingdon Press, 1996.

Talley, Thomas J. *The Origins of the Liturgical Year*, 2nd ed. Collegeville, MN: Liturgical Press, 1986.

Webber, Robert E. *Ancient-Future Time: Forming Spirituality through the Christian Year.* Grand Rapids, MI: Baker Books, 2004.

Webber, Robert E. *Ancient-Future Worship: Proclaiming and Enacting God's Narrative.* Grand Rapids, MI: Baker Books, 2008.

# BIBLIOGRAPHY


Athanasius, Saint (373). *On the Incarnation*, trans. John Behr. Yonkers, New York: St. Vladimir's Seminary Press, 2011.

*The Book of Common Prayer*. New York: Oxford University Press, 2007.

Cherry, Constance M. *The Worship Architect: A Blueprint for Designing Culturally Relevant and Biblically Faithful Services*. Grand Rapids, MI: Baker Academic, 2010.

Galli, Mark. *Beyond Smells and Bells: The Wonder and Power of Christian Liturgy*. Brewster, MA: Paraclete Press, 2008.

Howard, Thomas. *Evangelical Is Not Enough: Worship of God in Liturgy and Sacrament*. San Francisco, CA: Ignatius Press, 1984.

Smith, James K. A. *You Are What You Love: The Spiritual Power of Habit*. Grand Rapids, MI: Brazos Press, 2016.

Stubbs, David L. "Ethics." In *A More Profound Alleluia*, ed. Leanne Van Dyk, 133–153. Grand Rapids, MI: Wm. B. Eerdmans Publishing Co., 2005.

Webber, Robert E. *The Divine Embrace: Recovering the Passionate Spiritual Life*. Grand Rapids, MI: Baker Books, 2006.

White, James F. *Documents of Christian Worship: Descriptive and Interpretive Sources*. Louisville, KY: Westminster John Knox Press, 1992.